Adulting

THE ULTIMATE CHEAT SHEET

Adulting

THE ULTIMATE CHEAT SHEET

HALEY CAVANAGH

CFI
An imprint of Cedar Fort, Inc.
Springville, Utah

© 2024 Haley Cavanagh
All rights reserved.

No part of this book may be reproduced in any form whatsoever, whether by graphic, visual, electronic, film, microfilm, tape recording, or any other means, without prior written permission of the publisher, except in the case of brief passages embodied in critical reviews and articles.

This is not an official publication of The Church of Jesus Christ of Latter-day Saints. The opinions and views expressed herein belong solely to the author and do not necessarily represent the opinions or views of Cedar Fort, Inc. Permission for the use of sources, graphics, and photos is also solely the responsibility of the author.

Paperback ISBN 13: 978-1-4621-4640-6
ebook ISBN 13: 978-1-4621-4764-9

Published by CFI, an imprint of Cedar Fort, Inc.
2373 W. 700 S., Suite 100, Springville, UT 84663
Distributed by Cedar Fort, Inc., www.cedarfort.com

Library of Congress Registration Number: 2024930003

Cover design by Shawnda Craig
Cover design © 2023 Cedar Fort, Inc.
Edited and Typeset by Liz Kazandzhy

Printed in the United States of America

10 9 8 7 6 5 4 3 2 1

Printed on acid-free paper

In loving memory of Amy Lee Cahoon,
who brought warmth and light to everyone.

CONTENTS

Acknowledgments ... viii

Introduction ... 1

1: Finances ... 3

2: Cleaning ... 27

3: Cooking ... 37

4: Health Care ... 59

5: Everyday Hacks ... 69

6: Home Remedies ... 83

7: Beauty Treatments ... 93

8: Traveling ... 103

9: Life Advice ... 113

10: Parenting ... 137

11: Survival ... 147

Afterword ... 157

Notes ... 158

About the Author ... 160

ACKNOWLEDGMENTS

I WANT TO THANK THE FOLLOWING PEOPLE FOR THEIR HELP AND SUPPORT in the creation of this book:

- The editors at Cedar Fort Publishing for their insightful feedback and guidance.
- Dru Huffaker and Shawnda Craig for believing in this book and for their tireless work in getting it published.
- Bianca Duarte and Robin Johnson for their illustration work and cover art.
- My family and friends for their love and support throughout this journey. Esmé and Emmeline, I love you so much, and raising you has been my ultimate joy.

I would also like to thank the following teachers and parents for influencing my life through our shared experiences and lessons, which helped shape the content of this book:

- Carole and Rod Cavanagh
- Drill Sergeant Dennis Davis
- Don Durkee
- Esther Adams
- Glenda Gunn
- Holly Rundman
- Jaelann Call
- Justine Smith
- Karen Whiting
- Kyle Lewis
- Marilyn Gallant
- Mark Miller
- Mary and James Root
- Pamela Wilkey
- Paul and Carey Dubois
- Reva Lee Miller

Finally, I would like to thank the reader for picking up this book. Please know that a lot of love, preparation, and care went into the advice you're about to read—with you *specifically* in mind. I hope you find this book helpful and informative as you move forward. Remember, you are worthy of love and success. Never stop believing in your dreams.

INTRODUCTION

IF I COULD TRAVEL BACK IN TIME AND OFFER MY YOUNGER SELF ONE piece of advice, it would be this: Stay positive. You're doing better than you think you are.

Though the future might look uncertain and you don't know what's around the bend, your dreams, goals, and sunny outlook will be there to protect you through seemingly insurmountable obstacles.

Having said that, let's get real for just a second. One universal truth you can count on is that life loves to throw you curveballs, whether you're ready to hit them or not.

When I was sixteen, I rented a basement studio apartment owned by an older woman named Esther. Esther was my best friend's grandmother who kindly took me under her wing. I was broke, alone, scared, and worried about finishing high school. I had no idea what would happen. But for the first time in my life, I felt like I was in control of my destiny, free from abuse and negativity.

That moment was my earliest recollection of feeling like a real adult.

We all have different experiences that shape us into adults. Whether you leave home early or late, for good reasons or bad, adulthood is a time of great change and uncertainty. It's important to be prepared for the challenges and opportunities that lie ahead. Remember, there is no one right way to be an adult. The most important thing is to be true to yourself and to always keep learning and growing.

This book began as a few paragraphs I scratched together on a Post-it Note when I was pregnant with my first child—just advice I meant to teach my children when they were old enough. I started on my own much younger than I'd have liked. I wanted to pass on pearls of wisdom I'd learned firsthand to my daughters, both from life experience as a young adult and from my service in the military. Over the years, I pieced this book together with the same attitude until it took a definite shape. I realized the knowledge inside this book could benefit many others going through similar situations.

The chapters in this book offer you practical advice about making it on your own and good mental habits that will help you succeed in the long run. Please note that the advice in this book is geared toward those beginning life as adults. We start with the basics—not which high-speed lava lamp you're planning to buy at a posh home furnishing store. The ground-level info here is not meant to demean anyone's intelligence, social status, or income. Rather, it's to help you in your journey to become stable, functional, autonomous, and prosperous.

People tend to move out of their family's house somewhere in their late teens to late twenties. Whether or not you moved of your own volition, on good or bad terms, you now face the world's uncertainty. Some people are more prepared than others. Some struggle day to day. But when you get organized, find a method to your madness, and discover your unique rhythm, life becomes more manageable and fun!

By having a realistic outlook on what to expect and knowing how to manage and take care of yourself, you can have a more positive transition into adulthood and fully embrace your independence.

I hope this book helps you and benefits you in your journey.

Best of luck!

Haley Cavanagh

1

"Beware of little expenses. A small leak will sink a great ship."

—Benjamin Franklin [1]

Let's face it. Total financial freedom is attractive.

The independence of jumping in your car, driving wherever you wish, and visiting exciting places with minimal hassle is ideal. Then the reality sets in. You're strapped for cash. You don't have money for gas or food. You need to map out where you're going and determine your exit. You must schedule time off work, save for a hotel, and save a little on the side for expenses. The trip's not *impossible*—it's just more complex than you imagined.

While it's tempting to throw caution to the wind and go on a trip you can't afford, or buy that super rad Han-Solo-in-carbonite waffle maker you've had your eye on, if you do, you'll be in trouble.

You can have a wonderful, enjoyable life, even on a tight budget. By being financially stable and sticking to a solid budget, you can have the freedoms and adventures you crave, and those dreams can become a reality. But first comes responsibility. Be willing to be frugal and prioritize your expenses. Here are some pointers to help.

There are four good debts that are okay to have and progressively pay off in one's lifetime:

1. Student loans for college. Don't go over $20,000—find a job that offers tuition reimbursement and apply for grants or scholarships.
2. Mortgages
3. Car loans
4. Hospital payments (having a baby, necessary operations, etc.)

Helpful hint: The military will pay for 100 percent of college.

Avoid credit cards and overspending, and your credit and financial life will flourish. Stay away from payday loan places. They are money pits. Steer clear of them at all costs.

Debt is like a river—it's easy to fall into and get swept away but hard to get free. Working to get out of debt is like swimming in tar, and it adds a significant amount of stress to your life. If you want to buy something nice or go on a trip, save up for it. If you'd like money for an upcoming road trip, put aside $50 each paycheck, and within a year, you'll have over $1,000.

Budget at Least Six Months Ahead

Each January, plan your annual budget so you're never unprepared. Budget beforehand for holidays like Christmas and birthdays, school pictures and clothes, and trips. It helps to do a weekly or biweekly template of your expenses according to when they are due and copy and paste it for each payday.

Sit Down and Plan It Out

If you get paid biweekly, break the mortgage or rent payments into two. If your rent or mortgage portion is $830 a month, set aside $415 each

CHAPTER 1: FINANCES

paycheck to have other money for groceries, bill payments, going out to eat or to the movies, and so on.

Live Within or Below Your Means

Consumers average $340 in overspending each week. To the average person paying bills and carving their way through college one semester at a time, that can seem enormous. But it's all too easy to lose track of where your money goes until you realize you don't have any more.

Marriages and relationships have failed because of financial stress and credit card debt. Make good decisions and you'll be squared away.

Take advantage of free community places like libraries and parks. Parks often have basketball and tennis courts, volleyball pits, and running trails. Enjoy nature as often as possible if you live near mountains, hiking trails, walking paths by rivers, or the beach. It's free and fun! Spending more time in nature clears the cobwebs out, and it's a simple way to improve your mood and mental clarity.

The 50/30/20 Rule

The 50/30/20 rule[2] is a well-known, generic, easy budgeting method. The basic rule of thumb is to divide your after-tax income into three spending categories: 50 percent for needs, 30 percent for wants, and 20 percent for savings or paying off debt. The 30 percent for wants include things like eating out at restaurants with friends, going to the movies, skiing, or swimming. Your rent/mortgage and other necessary bills shouldn't be over 50 percent of your after-tax budget. Spread out your rent or mortgage payments across your biweekly or weekly paychecks. This way, it's easier to pay on time without sacrificing your essential needs. You'll have more cash for groceries and other necessities.

One way to whittle down your "wants" expenses is with online deals like Groupon and local websites that offer up to 80 percent off certain activities like bowling, concerts, or paint night. Buying a single, couple, or family annual membership to the zoo, aquarium, museum, or botanical garden often costs between $65 and $200. It will usually pay for itself after one or two visits, putting more money in your pocket and offering you a wonderful experience. Check out movie nights in the park in the summertime since they are often free and all you need to bring is a good blanket and snacks.

Pay Down as Much Debt as Possible

As you whittle down your debts, you will have more financial freedom to do what you want, when you want, and where you want. Paying down debt frees you financially and improves your credit score.

Make Smart Financial Choices

When spending your money, consider the following:

- Do I really need this?
- Can I afford what I want and not have it upset my budget?
- Could my money be better spent?

How to Set Up Utilities and Services

Contact electricity, water, gas, and internet services before you move. Research local providers for your utilities. Commercial apartments will have a list of the companies you should contact. Compare these places' plans, prices, and reviews to make informed decisions. Contact the providers to switch on the accounts; give information such as ID, proof of address, and contact details; and take note of due dates to avoid late fees. Keep track of usage and periodically review the plans. Procrastination can lead to unnecessary inconveniences and delays in your goal to settle into the home, so get the power, water, and gas turned on as soon as possible. As you plan and stay organized, you will manage bills and utilities like a pro.

CHAPTER 1: FINANCES

How to Pay Bills

With the modern conveniences we have today, paying bills is a lot easier than it was for our parents. You can pay bills "the old-fashioned way" (sending a money order or check in the mail), pay over the phone, or pay online through the convenience of your phone, tablet, or computer. If you'd like to receive your statements electronically, let your power, gas, or utility company know and they will stop sending paper statements. Find out which method you prefer.

Don't ignore bills. Keep track of all invoices received in a budgeting document and open them as soon as you get them. Keep a calendar on your wall or phone, write down when they're due, know how much you owe, and work it into your budget. Also, go online and look at your accounts.

Some bills like gas and power offer budget plans for a fixed rate year-round, saving you money if you intend to stay in your apartment or house longer than a year. Budget plans can also help guard against inflation during uncertain times if you have one locked in.

Select what's right for you. If you're doing well with your budgeting, you can opt in to bill autopay, where the bill will be deducted from your bank account monthly. If you don't select autopay, try to pay the invoice seven to ten days before it's due and stay on top of your payments. Look for ways to trim down costs to make your accounts more manageable, and pay attention to seasonal savings offers from your utility and power companies.

Health Insurance

Health insurance is no longer just a priority—it's now a legal requirement. You will need health, dental, eye, life, and 401k plans. When you're hired at a job and handed a benefits package, read your benefits extensively and decide what the best options are for you (and your family). Flexible spending accounts (FSAs) are smart, but not everyone understands how they work.

7

If your job offers an FSA account in their benefits package, put a small amount of each paycheck toward it and keep your FSA card handy. Your company will often match your contribution. If you have to go to the emergency room or urgent care because of a car crash or injury, your FSA card can pay for the visit's deductible when it's time, saving you hundreds of dollars.

You can also use FSA toward outpatient hospital visits, medical expenses, dental work, and prescriptions. You should never use your FSA card for anything unrelated to doctor's visits or medical issues. Keep an envelope of your itemized medical receipts, as FSA companies audit transactions and occasionally ask for documentation.

Pets

Our fur babies are our proxy children and must be well provided for and nurtured. If you own a cat or dog, invest in pet health insurance and a wellness plan for regular checkups. Animals develop health problems as they age, and veterinarians offer preventative care plans that will save you a significant amount in shots and treatment costs. Give your pets fresh food and water, and be sure to walk, train, clean, and play with them.

If you're buying a dog for the first time, try adopting one from the local animal shelter. Be aware that purebred dogs are more prone to illnesses and live shorter lives than mixed breeds. Mixed breeds are generally healthier. Consider if you can handle a puppy or not. Puppies gnaw on furniture as their teeth grow, and they need space to run around and a lot of love and attention. If you are timid in this area, try adopting an older, calmer dog instead. Keep your dogs well-groomed and investigate nearby pet resorts.

Never leave your animal unattended if you plan to be gone overnight or longer.

Filing Your Taxes

Unless you're an accounting wiz and know how to file tax returns online, it's best to get your taxes done at reputable agencies (such as Jackson

Hewitt or H&R Block). They offer protection against possible issues with your taxes, they can give you good advice, and they do not overcharge. If you're single, it's best to claim zero allowances on your taxes when you're hired at a job. That way, you get more money back during tax returns.

File your taxes as soon as you have all your W-2 statements and necessary information. Don't put it off until the last minute. The best time to file is around late January or early February. If you own a home, keep receipts for any tax-deductible improvements such as paint, rooftop repair, new water heaters, or energy-efficient installments to the house. Take the receipts with you when you file your taxes.

Resume Building

It's a competitive world out there, and one thing you can do career-wise is to keep your resume up to date. Have you learned a new software program or acquired skills through night classes or on-the-job training? Update your resume to reflect your current skill set. If you need help, visit the library and search online, or you can go to the Department of Workforce Services where many support avenues are available.

Car Oil Maintenance

Do you get worried when any of the little dashboard lights on your car indicate a problem with your engine or need an oil change? You're not alone.

To avoid those little dashboard lights and headaches, change the oil in your car every three months or 3,000 miles. If you don't know how to change the oil in a car or prefer to have a professional handle it, go to an oil change garage. If you're a service member in the military or going to college, ask about student or military discounts. Jiffy Lube usually offers veterans a free oil change every Veteran's Day. Hold on to oil change coupons as you see them come in the mail.

Learn how to change a tire. (You can watch instructional videos on YouTube or even ask the mechanic at your local garage to give you a quick rundown.) Check the air filter and windshield wipers on your car. Most garages will do this for you for free. Be polite with the attendants; they will generally want to help you. Check the tread in your tires and get them rotated every six months. Get new tires put on at least every two years, and invest in all-weather tires if you live in snow-laden climates.

Invest in off-road assistance like AAA and keep the phone number for a local tow truck company handy. Don't take chances on the road, and *never* drive distracted. If you need to use your phone or text, pull off the road somewhere safe, park, and turn off the engine. Always go the speed limit and stay aware of what's happening around you.

Off-Road Assistance

In addition to having car insurance, obtaining a membership to off-road assistance organizations (like AAA) will help if you ever become stranded while in your car. Off-road membership can cover towing, emergency gas delivery, tire changes, hotel travel discounts, car rentals, and theme parks. They also sometimes offer life insurance and many benefits for their members.

> *Helpful Hint:* If your engine light comes on, instead of heading directly to the nearest garage, go to an auto parts store to use a free code reader or OBD-II. The OBD-II is a diagnostic device you can plug into your driver's side dashboard. It will check the engine error codes or OBD-II PID service codes. Most auto parts stores offer this. Going this route will save you both time and money in diagnosing what's happening with your car. Evaluating the code error will enable you to make the best financial decisions to fix your vehicle without getting charged at a garage.

Cell Phones

To manage finances, saving money on cell phones is essential. Cell phone markets are ever-changing, and the moment you get a new phone, another one will come out. Find other ways to spend money better. Consider a used or refurbished phone instead of a brand-new one. These phones are significantly cheaper and have much of the same functionality.

Choose a prepaid or non contract plan to help avoid long-term commitments and unnecessary fees. Compare different service providers and their offerings. Don't upgrade to the latest model every year, as older models still provide good features at a lower charge. If you have an old phone, sell or trade it in to help pay for a new one. When you adjust finances and make little compromises, you will save money and still have an excellent cell phone.

Eyeglasses

Obtaining affordable eyeglasses is a challenge for many young adults. Here are tips to help you along the way:

- **Schedule an eye exam.** Make an appointment with an optometrist or eye clinic that offers affordable or discounted eye exams, and obtain an up-to-date vision prescription from them.
- **Shop around.** Compare different eyewear providers. In your eye exam, ask the optician's assistant if there's an option to pay for a printout of the prescription and explore different options. Prices vary, so before you settle on a pair of eyeglasses, check physical stores and online retailers for the best deals.
- **Consider online retailers.** Eyewear retailers often offer lower deals than traditional brick-and-mortar stores. Search for online retailers with good reviews that provide accurate prescription lenses and a wide selection of frames.
- **Look into available discounts.** Dig for discounts or promotions offered by retailers online and in person. Some eyewear retailers provide student discounts, promo codes, or special offers for first-time buyers.
- **Check with insurance.** If you have vision insurance, read through the policy to understand the benefits. Certain insurance plans will pay a fixed amount for lenses and frames or offer allowances or discounts for prescription eyewear. This applies to most online retailers as well.

- **Opt for basic frames.** While everyone wants their glasses to look cool, designer frames come with a hefty price tag. Select a basic, durable, no-frills frame. Accessorize the glasses and personalize or coat them later.
- **Check local resources.** If there are any local charities or organizations that offer discounted or free eyeglasses for individuals in need and you qualify, utilize them.
- **Think about secondhand or refurbished options.** Secondhand or refurbished eyewear sold at in-person retailers or online platforms are often in good condition and give you a great alternative.
- **Properly maintain your glasses.** Take care of your eyeglasses to prevent frequent replacements and extend their life. Keep them clean, store them in a protective case when you don't wear them, and avoid placing them face-down on flat surfaces.
- **Have a backup plan.** Purchase a backup pair of eyeglasses when feasible. Plan for future damage or loss, and ensure you have a spare set.

Your vision health is a priority. You will find suitable eyeglasses if you seek affordable options and prioritize quality.

Home Buying

The housing market has undergone radical changes in the last ten years alone. First-time home buyers face insurmountable challenges getting into homes. They often must put $70,000–$80,000 down, and fewer homes are for sale. If you are in the military, opt for a VA home loan, which allows you to not put anything down.

It's an admittedly frustrating time for home buyers, but if you do buy a home, *always* follow the 30/30/3 rule:[3]

- Rule #1: Spend no more than 30 percent of your gross income on a monthly mortgage payment. Thirty percent is a tough pill for many people who want the home of their dreams. But realistically, you'll foreclose within a year if you get into a house you can't afford.

CHAPTER 1: FINANCES

- Rule #2: Save at least 30 percent of the home value in cash or semi-liquid assets.
- Rule #3: Limit your target home's value to three times your annual household gross income.

Refinancing

After you have a mortgage and a car for a few years, one thing to think about is refinancing. You can set a great goal to see what expenses you can cut down so that you're not struggling after you pay your bills. For example, in 2016, one veteran's monthly mortgage payment was $1,250. With an interest rate reduction loan from the VA, the owners refinanced it to $835 a month after escrow. (This was for a large, four-bedroom home, but thanks to refinancing, it cost less than a low-end, one-bedroom apartment costs to rent these days.) The owners were then free to go on vacation, buy a car, spend money, and pay their bills on time.

Look for ways you can save on bills. Most power companies offer a Cool Keeper program. They will lock in the accounts for one fixed monthly price if you go energy-efficient or invest in solar panels. A Cool Keeper program has several advantages: it shaves down your monthly bill, makes for predictable long-term budgeting, and benefits the environment.

Set aside time to read literature on your gas, power, internet, cable, and water bills, which often will come in the mail. The companies will give their customers sound advice to save money, benefit them financially, and help the environment. Take advantage of seasonal programs designed to help you decrease amounts over holidays. Always have a mindset of how you can save more.

Budgeting

You can use any leftover money for recreation. The most important thing is that you have food in the house and that the bills are paid and up to date before you spend anything. Here is an example of how to budget on a biweekly income:

ADULTING: THE ULTIMATE CHEAT SHEET

BIWEEKLY BUDGET

EXAMPLE PAY PERIOD 1 - 1ST TO 17TH OF EACH MONTH

DUE BY:	SOURCE	CATEGORY	AMOUNT
17TH	GAS BILL	BILLS	100.00
17TH	POWER BILL	BILLS	115.00
1ST	RENT PORTION	HOUSING	850.00
N/A	FOOD AND GAS	HOUSING	300.00
N/A	RECREATION	PERSONAL	130.00

EXAMPLE PAY PERIOD 2 - 17TH TO 31ST OF EACH MONTH

20TH	CELL PHONE	BILLS	100.00
20TH	NETFLIX/PRIME	BILLS	20.00
N/A	FOOD AND GAS	HOUSING	300.00
18TH	CABLE/NET	BILLS	160.00
23RD	SIRIUS RADIO	PERSONAL	23.00
28TH	GYM/YOGA	PERSONAL	50.00
29TH	CAR PAYMENT	BILLS	300.00
29TH	CAR INSURANCE	BILLS	75.00
N/A	RECREATION	PERSONAL	100.00

Helpful Hint: To have a set schedule, write down the date of the month when each bill and payment is due, and maneuver your finances according to when you get paid.

A good rule of thumb is that your rent should *never* be more than 30 percent of your total individual (or collective) income. For example, if you made $18 an hour and worked full-time, your monthly income would be about $2,880. That means your individual rent/mortgage portion shouldn't be over $864 a month (30 percent of $2,880). Having a responsible roommate to share the costs can help you stay financially comfortable.

Don't be afraid to make little positive changes, especially those that will benefit your financial and overall health. It's worth it.

Generating Passive Income

Passive income means the ability to earn money with minimal effort and time, which helps people who scramble paycheck to paycheck turn things around and have a surplus of income. In today's fast-paced world, passive income offers financial stability, flexibility, and the potential for wealth accumulation.

There are multiple ways to earn passive income:

1. Invest in dividend stocks. Company dividend stocks provide a steady stream of passive income with fair consistency. Company shares distribute a portion of their profits to shareholders regularly. Research and invest in well-established companies with consistent dividend payments. When reinvesting dividends, you compound earnings and increase passive income over time.

2. Open an online business. There are countless opportunities for young adults to generate passive income online, whether they have an e-commerce store, create or sell digital products, or have a successful blog or YouTube channel. To start an online business, you would need to set up an account and add content. Lucrative online businesses generate income through advertisements, sales, and royalties.

3. Invest in real estate. Consider buying a home or rental property to earn passive income through rent or sublet. Read through the loan rules and regulations and contact your lender beforehand to be aware of stipulations.

4. Leverage intellectual property. Do you have a creative talent or expertise in a particular field? Leverage intellectual property and generate passive income as you earn royalties. Go nuts. Write a book, record a music track or audiobook, and stay aware of your intellectual property rights as you move forward.

Passive income can help put food on the table and pay a few bills when times are tough. Explore the different passive income avenues and discover which is right for you. Do something you love and reap the benefits as they compound over time.

Retirement Planning

The standard retirement age in the United States is between sixty-two and seventy. You may not be able to work for as long as you think, so it's never too early to plan for retirement. Many people end up retiring much earlier due to health issues or disabilities. Take advantage of HR fairs and retirement discussion opportunities to learn about 401ks and Roth IRAs.

By putting aside 3 percent of your income each paycheck in a 401k, you can secure a substantial nest egg when you are old enough to retire.

The longer you save, the more squared away you'll be since investments compound over time. You can choose from various investment portfolios, from safe and stable to diversified and high-risk. Index funds are less risky and have a steady history of high returns. Most companies will match your 401k contribution, increasing your retirement savings.

Think long and hard about where you want to be when you're sixty-five, and start planning for your future today! The earlier you start investing, the more it will compound and grow as you get older, maturing right along with you. If you switch jobs, you can roll over your 401k account to your new organization.

> *Helpful hint:* Stock markets can take a hit in unprecedented times, such as during the Great Recession or the 2020 COVID-19 pandemic. If you've got a 401k, lock it into a stable portfolio when the market gets shaky. Once things settle down, mix up your investments to diversify your portfolio for more flexibility.

Change Is Good

Change can be scary, but it should not be feared. Always look for ways to save money and cut costs. See if there's a way to get that power bill down. Find a more affordable internet plan. Pack lunches and drinks for work or out on the weekends instead of buying fast food. Eat out sparingly. Develop a healthy, budget-conscious mindset and stick to it.

Don't Expect Handouts

In an entitled generation, not expecting handouts is a challenging concept for many people, but it's necessary in order to be truly independent as an adult. If you are one of the lucky ones with supportive parents who enjoy helping you every step of the way, congratulations! Honor and respect them. Otherwise, from this point forward, assume everything is on you. Take care of yourself, spend wisely, and be careful with your money. It's up to you to keep track of your budget and take care of expenses. The wiser your choices, the less you'll have to worry or struggle.

How to Balance a Checkbook

With the convenience of online banking and debit cards, we now write fewer checks than usual. But those with checks need to know how to balance their checkbook. By balancing your checkbook, you can keep track of what goes in and what comes out, avoid going overdrawn, and spot mistakes.

Here's how you can do this:

1. Write down all transactions in your checkbook register, including deposits, withdrawals, card purchases, bill payments, and wire transfers.
2. Compare your monthly account statement and online register to your checkbook. Scout out any transactions that do not match.
3. Adjust your checkbook to reflect current transactions.
4. Keep your checkbook balanced so you're aware of your spending habits and can make sure that what's in your checkbook matches your online monthly statements.

Even though banks offer overdraft protection, and you should certainly sign up for it, always keep your bank balance positive. Only write checks when you've budgeted and know there's money available.

Credit Scores

Your credit report is a record of all your credit history. Your credit score reflects the information in your credit report. It is based on purchases, length of accounts, and payment histories. Your credit score affects your loan eligibility and how much you have to pay for that loan.

Many factors determine your credit score, including whether you pay your bills on time and how much you owe to creditors and debts. Your credit score fluctuates and can change depending on how your credit history changes, like if you buy a home, take out a car loan, or refinance a debt.

Build a good credit score, always pay your bills on time, and pay off your debts as much as possible. The better your credit score, the better your loan payment or interest rate offer will be. Your credit score can also determine how much your interest rate will be when you get a mortgage. Take advantage of perks from your bank account online. Most banks will allow you to check your credit score online for free weekly. Some will also show you summaries of your spending habits to help you better budget within your means.

Building and Improving Your Credit Score

Many lender decisions revolve around your credit report, so don't open more accounts than you need. Newer accounts indicate a more significant risk. As you age, your older accounts will reap the benefits. Use credit responsibly and make payments on time. After successful account management, you can seek increases to your credit limit.

Try to pay a little more each time you pay a bill. For example, if you have a car payment of $250, try paying an extra $20 each month. Little tweaks like this help improve credit scores and reduce your costs and interest.

Pay bills on time every month. This is crucial for maintaining a good credit score. Keep low balances on your accounts and pay them down. Settle any overdue payments promptly and ensure future payments are made on time. This will gradually improve your credit score.

Making real estate payments will reduce a portion of your outstanding principal balance, benefiting your score. Take opportunities to pay down balances on your real estate accounts.

Grocery Shopping

Make a grocery list ahead of time. Download coupons particular to your store before shopping. If you shop at Walmart or Kroger, it helps to

Chapter 1: Finances

download coupons you know you'll use and then apply them at checkout. With multiple options like pickup, in-store purchasing, and delivery, you can choose whichever method you prefer.

Shop with a Calculator

Shopping with a calculator can help you stay on a budget. When shopping for groceries in person, use your phone to track expenses or try the scan-as-you-go method. Prepare a list in advance, detailing each item's cost and anticipated tax to stay on target. If you add to your calculator as you add items to your cart, you won't be surprised by the amount at checkout.

The Dollar Store

Even if you're doing fantastic financially, it's smart to use a dollar store to get certain non-perishable goods, cleaning products, and random items, such as the following:

- Cleaning sponges and scouring pads
- White vinegar
- General seasonings (salt and pepper)
- Instant hot chocolate
- Q-tips
- Toothpaste, floss, and mouthwash
- Hydrogen peroxide
- Baking soda
- Freezer and sandwich bags
- Lint rollers
- Aluminum foil
- Saran wrap

- Cleaning products (for the bathroom and kitchen)
- Garbage bags
- Paper products (plates, cups, etc.)
- Party decorations and balloons
- Bottled water and juice
- Tupperware and kitchenware
- Arts and crafts
- Christmas decorations
- Non-perishable candy and snacks

You can shave up to $50 off your monthly grocery bill by shopping for these items at the dollar store. The products will have the same quality as store-bought brands while saving you money. It's a great way to save pocket or vacation money.

Stay smart. Even if you're rolling in the Benjamins, keep clipping those coupons from the mail for restaurants, grocery stores, and so on.

If you're struggling with a highly tight grocery budget, you might want to look into a nearby food bank. Before you do, grocery shop first for cost-effective, staple-solid healthy foods, such as the following:

- Rice and soy sauce
- Oatmeal
- Chicken breast
- Beef (lean)
- Pork
- Bread
- Pastas (spaghetti, rotini, penne, etc.)
- Eggs
- Potatoes
- Peanut butter
- Jam/jelly
- Apples
- Seasonal fruit on sale
- Baby carrots, bananas, lettuce, celery, onions, squash, yams
- Milk
- Canned corn and green beans
- Frozen fruit and veggies
- Ramen noodles (add veggies)
- Generic-brand soup
- Honey
- Condiments (ketchup, mayonnaise, etc.)
- Margarine
- Cereals high in fiber
- Sauces (spaghetti, tomato, Alfredo, etc.)
- Beans, lentils, and chickpeas
- Yogurt
- Spinach and peas

Head for the clearance sections first when you go to the grocery store. There are often great deals you can snag on items in good condition. Meal planning is a critical aspect of grocery shopping. Be creative in your choices and make the most of your food to stretch it out, portion it, and keep variety while maintaining your health.

Breakfast Ideas

- Cereal with milk and fruit
- Eggs, toast, and fruit
- Yogurt and fruit

Lunch Ideas

- Baked potatoes
- Sandwiches, soups, or salads
- Cereal or dinner leftovers
- Instant noodles with tuna or mixed veggies

Dinner Ideas

- Canned chicken and rice with sauce
- Hot dogs, mac and cheese, and veggies
- Pork chops with salad
- Spaghetti with sauce and salad
- Crock-Pot chicken with carrots and potatoes
- Mac and cheese with ground beef
- Tuna and rice casserole with veggies
- Baked potatoes, cheese, and beans
- Pizza with salad
- Chicken fajitas (with the tortillas and leftover Crock-Pot chicken)
- Frozen burritos with rice and veggies

Here is an example grocery list based on a weekly budget of $120 for two weeks (though prices obviously will vary over time):

- Oatmeal (1.75)
- Rice (1.50)
- Beans (canned or dry) (1.50)
- Lentils (canned or dry) (1.60)
- Canned tuna x 4 (4.00)
- Canned chicken x 2 (4.00)
- Eggs (3.00)
- Bread (1.60)
- Tortillas (2.00)
- Milk ½ gallon (2.60)

- Potatoes 5 lbs. (2.50)
- Carrots 1 lb. (1.00)
- Cabbage/lettuce (2.00)
- Cucumbers x 2 (1.25)
- Celery (1.60)
- Peanut butter (1.60)
- Popcorn (generic) (2.50)
- Frozen veggies x 3 (generic) (3.00)
- Instant noodles x 6 (1.75)
- Mac and cheese x 3 (3.00)

- Personal pizza (Totino's) (1.75)
- Hot dogs (1.70)
- Hot dog buns (generic) (1.60)
- Frozen burritos x 4 (generic) (2.00)
- Canned fruit and veggies x 3 (4.00)
- Pasta and sauce (2.70)
- Apples x 3 (3.00)
- Bananas x 6 (1.50)
- Oranges x 3 (2.25)
- Seasonal or clearance fruit (2.00)
- Applesauce (generic) (2.00)
- Chicken (whole) (7.00)
- Pork (5.00)
- Ground beef (5.00)
- Generic cereal (2.00)
- Yogurt x 4 (3.00)
- Cheese block 8 oz. (generic) (2.00)
- Tea bags or hot chocolate (1.25)
- Kool-Aid packets x 4 (1.00)
- Soups x 4 (4.00)
- Garbage bags (generic) (1.25)
- Toilet paper (generic) (6.00)
- Napkins (generic) (1.50)
- Shampoo and conditioner (VO5) (2.00)
- Bar soap (Dial or Dove) (1.00)
- Dish soap (generic) (1.50)
- Laundry detergent (5.00)
- Dryer sheets (generic) (2.75)

Helpful Hint: When shopping, choosing the generic brand can significantly shave money off your grocery bill. Use coupons.

Shop the Sales

Take advantage of in-store "4 for $4.00" or "5 for $5.00" sales, also known as red- or blue-sticker sales, and use coupons if you have them. Large chain stores like Kroger or Walmart often do a deal where you can buy four or five participating items. You'll save an additional $5.00 if you buy specific brands.

Buy as many sale items on your list as possible. Use digital and physical coupons at checkout, shaving off even more. Be sure to check that the on-sale price is lower than what you budgeted for while shopping. If it's not, stick to your original budget. You can save $50–$150 and eat well if you do it right.

Unless you're hosting regular dinner parties, buy cheap table napkins when shopping. Use the extra few dollars you would've spent to buy a quilted brand of toilet paper or toiletry item you prefer. By prioritizing and shifting things around to tailor to your lifestyle, you can live a comfortable, pleasant life, even on a budget.

Plan Your Meals

Take a few minutes before your work or school week to jot down what you will have for dinner each night the following week. Put it on your fridge, phone, or somewhere visible to have easy access. Don't be afraid to use a Crock-Pot. Slow cookers can be invaluable to aid you in less preparation time and alleviate the stress of cooking if you're busy. Being prepared will reduce stress and help you feel organized.

Check Out Online Deals

If you want to go out with friends somewhere recreational, be money-wise and look first at online deals. Subscribe to deal websites and newsletters.

Online vendors like Groupon, LivingSocial, and others feature recreational passes, grocery items, and dining-out deals. Use cash back and reward apps, which offer discounts and rewards when you shop online or in the store. Earn cash back on groceries, dining, and recreational passes if they're available through their partner merchants.

Scout for online group buying deals to shave a pretty penny off, and you and your friends can split the reduced price, which they'll appreciate. Group buying allows you to split the amount with friends or family and enjoy the experience together.

Follow the social media accounts of favorite recreational centers, restaurants, and supermarkets. Many of these places have flash sales, discounts, and promotions through social media. Stay in the loop to help you take advantage of these deals as they come along. Online marketplaces often offer discounted gift cards or vouchers for recreation, groceries, and restaurants, allowing you to save on purchases.

Take the time to compare rates and reviews to help you find the best deals and make informed choices.

If you're a student, take advantage of student discounts. Many stores and facilities offer special deals for students, which cuts off a significant portion. Look for online coupons and digital flyers from your favorite grocery stores before shopping. Some grocery store apps offer exclusive coupons you can utilize.

Read the terms and conditions, note coupons' expiration dates, and exercise caution when you enter personal information or make purchases online.

Ways to Save on Your Bills

Here are a few things you can do to whittle down your bills:

- Unplug any unused electrical devices. Unplug if you have a cell phone charging cable, kitchen appliance (e.g., toaster, air fryer), or other electronic device not in use. Phantom charges do occur when devices aren't in use. You can ensure you don't get charged by unplugging.
- Use power strips and timers to save power. Consider unplugging your TV while you're at work.
- Invest in solar window cling film to help reduce heat in the summer. Heat control film will reduce the heat from a window or screen by up to 90 percent.
- If you rent or own a home, compare the meter reading on your utility bill to what you see on your meter. If anything looks questionable, call your utility company and discuss it with them to avoid being overcharged.
- Reevaluate your cell phone bill and usage. Is your plan right for you? If you text more than you call, do you need unlimited calls? If your cell phone bill is high, consider using Zoom or Skype, which is free and offers face time with your loved ones and friends.
- Compare different internet and phone plans. Is there one with better ratings that happens to be more cost-efficient?

CHAPTER 1: FINANCES

- If you pay for your services separately, consider bundling your phone, internet, and cable services, as it may provide a better deal.
- Lower your cable bill or digital streaming service by canceling any channels or apps you don't watch. Consider downgrading to a package that better fits your entertainment needs and costs less.

MONTHLY BUDGET

MONTH OF

INCOME			
DATE	SOURCE	CATEGORY	AMOUNT

BILLS & FIXED EXPENSES		
DATE	SOURCE	AMOUNT

VARIABLE EXPENSES		
DATE	SOURCE	AMOUNT

SUMMARY	
SOURCE	AMOUNT
INCOME	
BILLS & FIXED EXPENSES	
VARIABLE EXPENSES	
BALANCE	

2

Cleaning

"Housekeeping ain't no joke."

—Louisa May Alcott [4]

Cleaning is like math—you either love it or you hate it. Either way, you must do it. While it's tempting to ignore those dirty dishes or let the laundry get extra wear and tear, the reality is that you have to keep it up.

Setting a schedule of chores and settling into a rhythm that works for you will help contribute to a clean, livable life, improving your mental health and overall quality of living.

Here are some helpful tips to simplify your cleaning regime if you're in the "I'd rather swallow dirty dish water than clean my house" camp.

Find Your Rhythm

Learning to keep your space clean is like dancing to an unfamiliar beat. It's strange at first, but the more you dance, the more you get to know the rhythm and the better you become.

The following guidelines can help:

1. Stick to a set cleaning schedule to prevent your home from getting too messy. Use the checklist at the end of this chapter to help.
2. Start small. Don't try to clean your entire home in one day, but focus on one room and one task at a time, with different days for different chores. Spread out the schedule so you don't get overwhelmed.
3. Delegate. If you have roommates, ask them to split the cleaning tasks to make the workload fair and help keep the house clean with less effort. You may also hire a cleaning service to help on occasion.
4. Invest in basic supplies like a vacuum, mop, broom, and dustpan. Use the right tools for the right chore.
5. Have fun. Turn on your playlist or audiobook and transform chores into fun activities. Cleaning has the potential to lessen stress, not the other way around.

Chores don't have to be a bore. Keep things fun and don't be afraid to ask for help. If you struggle to clean, enlist assistance from friends, family, or a professional service. Find your rhythm and try different methods to discover which suits your lifestyle and personality.

Above all, don't become discouraged. Cleaning is an ongoing task and seems never-ending, but remember, a little effort makes a big difference.

How to Do Laundry

Unless you have children or a lot of people in your house, pick one day a week to get the laundry done. Weekends are best. Read the tags on your clothes, and know which ones require special care or dry cleaning. Clean those clothes according to their care guidelines. Separate your whites from your colors. Don't overload either the washer or dryer.

When loading a washing machine, select the proper load size and use the right amount of detergent. On every detergent bottle, the inside of the cap will have three lines, often numbered, to differentiate between the size loads so you know how much to use.

Select a laundry detergent that agrees with your skin. You can select liquid, pods, or powder—whichever is most convenient for you. Liquid detergent works well on oil and grease stains and is affordable. Pods are lightweight and suitable for use, with a premeasured dose for each load, and they are popular and widely used. Powder detergent has been around for almost a hundred years. Powder detergent is the cheapest, and the formula is more stable than liquid or pods. It helps remove grass and mud stains.

Select a fragrance-free detergent or fabric softener for sensitive skin if you are prone to eczema, hives, itching, or skin irritation. Most brands have sensitive skin varieties. If your clothes smell, add a capful of white vinegar to each load to remove the stink.

Using a Washer

For most loads, use a permanent-press cycle unless the garments require delicate or gentle. Temperature-wise, cold water is best. Unless the clothes specify using warm water or you find that is what you prefer, clean with cold. Read the tags and decide what's best for you. The dryer heat removes all germs, so the washer's temperature doesn't make a difference in eliminating bacteria. Run the load for the cycle duration, remove it after the spin cycle stops, and put it in the dryer.

> *Helpful Hint:* By reading the tags on your clothes, you will know which clothes require line drying. If line drying isn't an option, you can put these items on a hanger and hang them on your bathroom shower rod or atop a doorjamb overnight.

Using a Dryer

Keep your dryer on a regular heat setting unless the tags for your clothing indicate otherwise. Add a dryer sheet (or two) to the load to prevent static. Check that the clothes are dry before removing them, then fold or hang up the clothes and put them away. Clean your dryer filter after each use. Remove and throw away all lint on the filter and replace it before starting a new load. Clean your exhaust vent once a year and wipe off the top of the dryer to remove any lingering lint or clothing dust. Iron and press clothes as necessary.

> *Helpful Hint:* The dollar store sells lint rollers. Buy one or two and keep them in the laundry area to remove any lint from clothes as you put them away. Use duct tape or a vacuum if you can't obtain a lint roller.

How to Keep a Clean Home

If you own or rent a home, there are several essential things you need to do to keep your home clean and free of infestation:

1. Change your air filters every three months. Dust and allergens can get into the house and make people sick during hay fever season or weather changes. Clean air filters prevent E. coli and the bacteria that cause the flu virus.
2. Check your smoke and carbon monoxide detector alarms monthly. Replace batteries twice a year, and make sure a carbon monoxide detector is in each bedroom.
3. Spray for insects (or use an organic-friendly company) every six months. Spraying will keep your home bug-free. Most apartments will do this for you. Check with your apartment manager. Seal your non-perishable foods in airtight containers and use ziploc bags to prevent infestation. Try to buy foods with an in-line ziploc.
4. Vacuum out your air vents. Cleaning your air vents will help make the air more breathable and allow fresh, clean air to circulate the vents without dust balls or debris. Using your hose on your vacuum, remove your air vent grills and vacuum them out. Make a habit of wiping light switches, countertops, and door handles

CHAPTER 2: CLEANING

with Clorox or Lysol wipes. Suppose you're bored with time to kill. Put on some music and sweep the floor. Be as productive as you can in your off moments.

5. Have a specialist or technician perform routine maintenance of your water heater.

6. Clean your bathroom(s) at least once or twice a week. Scrub your toilet frequently. Start beneath the bowl's rim to clean out any accumulated bacteria. After cleaning your toilet, dry your toilet brush by trapping it between the toilet seat lids. Drip drying will keep it more hygienic and prolong the life of the brush. Buy a new toilet brush every 3–6 months and dispose of the old one to keep your bathroom germ-free.

7. Keep your dishes clean and up to date as much as you can. Have fun cleaning the dishes. Plug in the earbuds, crank up your playlist, and let your imagination take flight as you wash up or stack the dishwasher in good spirits. Wipe your kitchen sink with disinfecting wipes or a cleaning product to prevent disease and keep you healthy. Sweep and mop your kitchen a few days a week.

8. Keep your counters and tabletops free of clutter. Stay up to date with your laundry so you always have clean clothes to wear. The less messy tabletops are, the easier it is to find things and the more organized you'll feel.

9. Keep your hardwood floors swept or vacuumed to avoid dust. Spot clean with disinfecting wipes if you don't have the time to mop or steam clean.

10. Every 3–6 months, buy new toothbrushes, hairbrushes, bath sponges, and toilet brushes. Use old toothbrushes to clean and old hair brushes for your 72-hour kit.

How to Defrost a Freezer

Defrost your freezer on an as-needed basis. Everyone's freezer gets frost buildup at some point. You have a few ways you can defrost a freezer. You can wait for the ice to melt, which can take a while. Or you can use a blow-dryer, hot spatula, or cloth to remove excess ice. Most people opt for the first method. To defrost your freezer, do the following:

1. Turn the freezer off.
2. Empty it.
3. Remove any drawers or detachable shelves.
4. Look for a drainage hose. Pull it forward and connect it to a longer hose if your freezer has one. You want to draw the water away from the freezer.
5. Lay old newspapers or towels in front of the freezer to catch the water.
6. Remove ice as it softens with either a spatula or a cloth. Never use a knife. Don't use your hand either because you can get freezer burn.
7. Clean and mop up the excess water. Keep a mop bucket handy next to the freezer to collect extra water.
8. Clean the freezer. Clean the walls and shelves of the freezer as best you can if you haven't done so before.
9. To prevent ice buildup, dry the freezer entirely before turning it back on.
10. Make sure the seal on the door is working.
11. Turn the freezer back on.

How to Remove Urine or Odors from a Mattress

If your child or pet wets the bed and you need to clean the mattress, you'll need paper towels, white vinegar, baking soda, and a vacuum. Perform the following steps:

1. Open a window in the bedroom to ventilate it, and turn on a ceiling fan if you have one.
2. Saturate the mattress (or the stain's area) with white vinegar. You can use a spray bottle to distribute it or drizzle it. If you drizzle it, do it sparingly so it doesn't seep through the mattress.
3. Using the paper towels, soak up the vinegar. Press several layers of paper towels down if needed.
4. Sprinkle baking soda all over the mattress. Let it sit for several hours, keeping the room well-ventilated. If the smell is terrible, leave it for three to four hours. After a few hours, it will begin to cake as it soaks up the vinegar, urine, and leftover odors.

CHAPTER 2: CLEANING

5. After at least two to three hours have passed, vacuum the mattress thoroughly. Make sure you repeatedly review the crevices to remove any leftover residue. It should be fresh and clean. If you desire, spray fabric refresher over it and put a mattress protector on it before replacing the bedsheets.

6. For sheets and bedding that have a foul smell, add a half cup of white vinegar to the laundry wash load to get the odor out.

How Often to Clean Certain Things

- Sheets: once a week
- Cars: every one to three weeks
- Dogs: as needed
- Jeans: every four to five wears
- Bras: every three to four wears
- Your face: every morning and night
- Your hair: every other day
- Bathrooms: once a week
- Bathtubs: twice a week or as needed
- Grout: once a year
- Window screens: once a year
- Mattress: every six months
- Windows: twice a year
- Fridge: once a month
- Oven: every six months
- Pots and pans: after every use
- Carpet: once a year
- Wood furniture: once a year
- Purse: every week
- Dishwasher: every month
- Washer and dryer: biweekly
- Bed Pillows: every three to six months
- Computers: as needed
- Sink: every day

Descale and Clean an Electric Kettle with Vinegar

1. Fill the kettle halfway with water and white vinegar in equal parts.
2. Bring the mixture to a boil.
3. Let the vinegar-water mix sit for 15–20 minutes. Unplug. Pour out the mixture and rinse the equipment, repeating the necessary steps for dirtier kettles.
4. Wipe the kettle inside with a clean cloth and leave it to dry completely.
5. After drying, boil water in the kettle and discard it to remove the possible remaining aftertaste.
6. If there is a lingering smell, boil water one or two times. If needed, repeat the steps and leave the solution in the kettle overnight, then rinse.

You can use a sponge to scrub the inside of the kettle. Always exercise caution when cleaning around the heating coil or element at the bottom.

Clean the outside of the kettle with dishwashing liquid, rinse, and wipe it with a clean damp cloth.

CLEANING CHECKLIST

KITCHEN & DINING AREA

- ○ Clean countertops
- ○ Clean sink and faucet
- ○ Dishwasher: clean outside and inside
- ○ Microwave: clean inside and outside
- ○ Oven: clean inside and outside
- ○ Refrigerator: clean outside and inside
- ○ Stove: clean top, front, and inside
- ○ Sweep and mop floor
- ○ Wipe down cabinets and drawers

LIVING ROOM

- ○ Clean baseboards
- ○ Clean ceiling fans
- ○ Clean windowsills
- ○ Dust blinds or curtains
- ○ Dust light fixtures
- ○ Dust surfaces (tables, shelves, etc.)
- ○ Fluff and arrange cushions
- ○ Vacuum or sweep floors
- ○ Vacuum upholstery (sofas, chairs)

MASTER BATHROOM

- ○ Change towels
- ○ Check exhaust fan
- ○ Clean counters, cabinets
- ○ Clean light fixtures
- ○ Clean sink and faucet
- ○ Clean toilets (including bowl, seat and base)
- ○ Clean walls and baseboards
- ○ Empty trash can
- ○ Scrub shower/tub (including tiles, grout, and showerhead)
- ○ Sweep and mop floor
- ○ Wipe down mirrors

MASTER BEDROOM

- ○ Clean baseboards
- ○ Dust blinds or curtains
- ○ Dust surfaces
- ○ Make bed
- ○ Vacuum or sweep floors

LAUNDRY

- ○ Clean washer and dryer
- ○ Organize and straighten items
- ○ Vacuum or sweep floors

3

"The only time to eat diet food is while you're waiting for the steak to cook."

—Julia Child [5]

IN A WORLD OF CONVENIENCE LIKE OURS, IT'S EASIER TO GRAB A VALUE meal at a drive-thru on the way home than to painstakingly create a meal when you're tired after a long day at work. But if you eat out more than you cook, you should rethink your approach and eat at home more often. Your wallet will thank you.

Cooking saves money, leads to a healthier and longer life, and gives you more autonomy. Most foods in restaurants are high in fat and calories, taking away from your natural energy. Cooking is a creative art and will provide you with an inspired outlet to turn simple, plain ingredients into beautiful, delicious dishes.

Here are a few menu items that are better to order when eating fast food or at restaurants:

- Chicken tenders or nuggets
- Lean turkey or fish sandwiches
- Salmon and rice
- Side salads with low-fat balsamic dressing
- Diet soda drinks or vitamin water
- Apple or orange slices

- Yogurt
- Steamed vegetables

Helpful Hint: If you order a grilled chicken sandwich from any fast-food restaurant, lay off the sauce to make it more nutritious.

Dieting

Eat at least two to three fruits and vegetables each day. Avoid fast food, but if you do get it, choose chicken tenders, fish, salad, or low-fat, high-protein foods.

Food is essential, and human beings need sustenance for their bodies and psyche. Don't start diets that greatly restrict your overall eating. Instead, opt for diets that are high in fiber and nutrients but are low in fat and calories. Drink plenty of water. Avoid too much caffeine. Make your health a priority, and remember that what you do today will set you up to be healthy and able-bodied twenty to thirty years down the road.

Helpful Hint: For a protein kick, boil three eggs for 25 minutes, soak them in cool water, remove the egg yolks, and enjoy the whites with a small pinch of salt. It will give you a protein boost of 12 grams without fat and only 45 calories.

High Fiber Protein Snacks

- Applesauce
- Kiwi fruit
- 1–3 egg whites
- Tomato
- Small clementine orange
- Sugar-free Jell-O
- Dill pickle
- Sugar-free hard candies
- High-fiber granola bars
- 12 Junior Mints
- 1 tsp. sunflower seeds
- Dried apricots or strawberries
- 5 cups 94% fat-free popcorn
- Baby carrots or celery with fat-free dressing

Expiration Dates: Check all expiration dates on milk, eggs, and perishable items. When shopping, reach for the milk at the back because it is often the freshest and most recently stocked. If you're unsure if something is expired, smell it before consuming it. Check that the fruit you intend to buy is free of bruises, bumps, and holes.

Use a Cutting Board

Do not cut meat, sandwiches, fruit, vegetables, or anything else directly on your kitchen counter or plate. Cutting on counters will lead to scratch marks, and if you rent an apartment, you will have to pay for it upon leaving. Buy a cutting board, use it, and scrub it with soapy water after each use. Wash all fruits and vegetables with water before consuming.

Knife Use

Use caution when you wield a knife. Cut *away* from the body with your hand atop the handle. Never place your skin beneath or next to the blade. Never point the knife in the direction of another person.

Cooking versus Microwaving

While convenient, microwaved food often doesn't taste as good as oven-cooked dinners. Microwaves admittedly save time, but try to cook your food in the oven whenever possible rather than nuke it. Microwaves heat the water molecules in food at an accelerated rate, producing uneven heating and making the food taste different. When food heats in an oven, the internal temperature is the same throughout the food as it cooks, so it tends to taste better.

How to Cook Meat

If you've never cooked meat before, the first thing to consider is what kinds of meat you eat. Are you a chicken, pork, beef, or fish person? Perhaps all the above?

Here are a few important things to remember when cooking meat:

- First, pay attention to internal cooking temperatures to avoid foodborne illnesses.
- Second, take the proper time to prepare and cook the meat thoroughly.

Invest in a digital, touch-free food thermometer to check the temperature of the meat. Select lean meat that looks healthy. Defrost your meat overnight in the fridge. Avoid defrosting meat in the microwave, as it can ruin the taste and texture. Do not thaw meat at room temperature or in the sink. Learn how to cut your meat. Trim extra fat with a boning knife.

You may choose to marinate your meat before cooking it. Make sure to seal it in a freezer bag and let it marinate for the correct time to tenderize the meat. Take the meat out of the fridge twenty to thirty minutes before cooking. Line a baking tray with aluminum foil and heat according to the temperature guidelines.

Follow the recommended temperatures and cooking times on the packaging for your meat. As you become used to cooking meat, you'll be able to tell if it looks cooked. Turn meat over at least once and ensure proper ventilation in your kitchen. Store your leftovers in a tightly sealed Tupperware container or freezer bag and consume them within three days.

Slow Cookers

Slow cookers are lifesavers if you work long hours and don't have much time to cook. And the great news is they come in all sizes. If you live alone, a small Crock-Pot could make the difference between coming home to a nice, warm meal and struggling to make something for yourself after a long, hard day. A larger Crock-Pot is the way to go if you live with others.

Most Crock-Pot meals take a mere few minutes of preparation, and by the time you get home from work or college, you'll have a warm, delicious dinner in the pot. You can also chuck twenty to thirty hot dogs in for two hours if you throw a party or barbecue and you'll be all set.

Slow cookers are a worthwhile investment and can introduce you to the world of cooking. You can buy used Crock-Pots at thrift stores to save a few dollars. There are countless slow cooker recipes online.

How to Make a Grilled Cheese Sandwich

Spray non-stick cooking spray on your stove top grill or a frying pan and heat the burner to medium. Spread margarine or butter on the outer side of two pieces of bread. Lay one piece of bread margarine-side down in the center of the grill or frying pan, and stack two cheese slices in the center. Cover with the other piece of bread, margarine-side up. Flip over and cook for two minutes on each side until the desired doneness. Serve and enjoy.

Helpful Hint: Grilled cheese sandwiches taste great with a side of tomato soup and basil.

Freeze Your Yeast

If you bake bread, you will need yeast. Yeast does have an expiration date, but it can remain fresh in the fridge for up to four months and in the freezer for six months to a year, with no need to thaw. The average "best by" date for typical yeast is two years.

Learn to Cook

There is a world of knowledge online and in the library with step-by-step instructions on cooking and making meals. You can make many meals with simple, cheap ingredients such as flour, sugar, salt, eggs, and oil. Take advantage of free instructional videos and teach yourself these skills. Or, if you already know how to cook, take it a step further and try cooking extraordinary dishes. Pasta machines are affordable, and it can be fun to make your own spaghetti or fettuccine.

Devote a week or so to learning how to cook simple meals. You will not only save money and contribute to your nutritional health, but you'll also build skills you can use for the rest of your life!

Corn on the Cob

Between June and September of each year, corn on the cob is in season, and it is *cheap*! Go to farmers' markets for great deals and the freshest produce. Buy a bunch of corn cobs from your favorite local grocery store or farmers' market, and experiment with the husks to get used to husking them fast. In high season, you can buy up to twenty cobs for only a few dollars, and it's possible to cook and store them in the freezer.

Helpful Hint: Corn on the cob tastes delicious sprinkled with Parmesan cheese or popcorn flavoring.

Regardless of where you are or what you end up doing, you must know how to prepare a meal for yourself and possibly others. Cooking is a necessary part of being an adult, and learning how to plan and create meals will keep you healthy and happy, and your wallet will thank you.

CHAPTER 3: COOKING

Helpful Recipes

DESSERTS

CHOCOLATE CHIP COOKIES

Prep Time: 20 Minutes
Makes: 48 cookies

Ingredients:

- 1 cup butter, softened
- 1 cup white sugar
- 1 cup packed brown sugar
- 2 eggs
- 2 tsp. vanilla extract
- 3 cups all-purpose flour
- 1 tsp. baking soda
- 2 tsp. hot water
- ½ tsp. salt
- 2 cups semisweet chocolate chips
- 1 cup chopped walnuts

Directions:

1. Preheat the oven to 350°F (175°C).
2. Cream together the butter, white sugar, and brown sugar until smooth.
3. Beat in the eggs one at a time, then stir in the vanilla.
4. Dissolve baking soda in hot water. Add to batter along with salt.
5. Stir in flour, chocolate chips, and nuts.
6. Drop large spoonfuls onto a parchment-lined cookie sheet or ungreased pans.
7. Bake for about 10 minutes or until the edges are nicely browned.

Delicious, Mouth-Watering Brownies

Ingredients:

- 1 cup soft butter
- 2 cups sugar
- ⅓ cup cocoa
- 4 eggs
- 1½ cups flour
- 2 tsp. vanilla
- ¼ tsp. salt
- 1½ cups chopped nuts (optional)
- 7-oz. jar of marshmallow crème
- 12 oz. chocolate chips
- 3 Tbsp. peanut butter
- 3 cups chocolate rice cereal

Directions:

1. Preheat the oven to 350°F.
2. Mix the butter, sugar, and cocoa in a mixing bowl.
3. Stir in the eggs.
4. Add the flour, vanilla, salt, and chopped nuts (optional).
5. Pour the mixture into a greased 1-inch deep baking sheet and bake at 350° for 20 minutes or until done.

Topping:

1. Spread marshmallow crème over cooled brownies. No need to put it back in the oven.
2. Combine chocolate chips and peanut butter in a small saucepan.
3. Cook over low heat, constantly stirring, and cook until melted and well blended.
4. Remove from heat and stir in the chocolate rice cereal.
5. Spread over the marshmallow layer, and let it cool in the fridge.

CHAPTER 3: COOKING

HOMEMADE CHOCOLATE TRUFFLES

Prep Time: 15 mins
Makes: 18 servings, 2 truffles each

Ingredients:

- 2½ pkg. semisweet chocolate (20 squares), divided
- 1 (8-oz.) pkg. cream cheese, softened
- Decorations: chopped cocktail peanuts, multi-colored sprinkles

Directions:

1. Melt 8 chocolate squares. Beat cream cheese with a mixer until creamy. Blend in melted chocolate. Refrigerate until firm.
2. Shape into 36 balls. Place on a waxed paper-covered baking sheet.
3. Melt the remaining chocolate. Use a fork to dip the truffles and return them to the baking sheet. Decorate with sprinkles or edible glitter, then refrigerate for 1 hour.

BREAKFASTS

Scrambled Eggs

Ingredients:

- 1–2 Tbsp. margarine
- 3 eggs
- ¼ tsp. salt
- ⅛ tsp. paprika
- 2 Tbsp. milk or cream

Directions:

1. Melt margarine in a skillet over low heat.
2. Mix the eggs, salt, paprika, and milk/cream separately. Be ready by the time the butter is hot and add the mixture, beaten with a fork until the eggs are uniform in color.
3. Begin on low-medium heat. As the eggs heat through, increase the heat, and with a spoon, shove the eggs about gently, but with accelerating speed, until they have thickened but are still soft.
4. Serve immediately. Makes two servings.

CHAPTER 3: COOKING

SOFT BOILED EGGS AND BREAD SOLDIERS (A.K.A. THE 4-MINUTE EGG)

Ingredients:

- 1–4 eggs
- Boiling water

Directions:

1. Fill a 2-quart saucepan with water and set it to boil. When the water is boiling over the water's surface, carefully lower an egg into the water with a slotted spoon and time for 4 minutes. For any additional eggs, add 1 minute each. For example, if you want to make 4 soft-boiled eggs, lower the eggs in boiling water and time for 7 minutes.
2. While boiling the eggs, put toast in the toaster. Once you make the toast, spread butter/margarine on it and slice into finger-sized portions. If you have a soldier cookie cutter, you can use that. Set aside.
3. When you've finished boiling the eggs, turn off the burner, and using a slotted spoon, transport the eggs to egg cups.
4. Tap your eggs in the following way: The pointed end facing up in the cup is the "top" of the egg you'll tap off. With the flat, broad face of a spoon, gently but firmly tap the top of the egg, creating a circular crack all around. Aim to make a "line" around the top third of the egg. Once you've created a circle of cracks, you can gently pry the top off with the edge of the spoon. Be careful not to apply too much force or else the shell could shatter and spread tiny fragments over your egg.
5. Discard the top, dip the bread soldiers into the yolk, and enjoy!

Eggies in a Basket

Ingredients:

- Butter or margarine
- 1–4 slices of bread
- 1–4 eggs

Directions:

1. Butter bread slices on both sides.
2. Cut an approximately 2-inch circle in the middle of each slice using a cookie cutter, egg cup, or shot glass.
3. Place buttered bread slices on a non-stick skillet or pan, preheated over medium heat.
4. Add a bit of butter or margarine around the edges of the pierced bread and crack your egg into the hole. Cook each side for 2 minutes, season, and enjoy.

Sunny Side Up Eggs

Ingredients:

- 1 Tbsp. olive oil or non-stick cooking spray
- 4 large free-range eggs
- ⅛ tsp. sea salt
- Freshly ground black pepper, to taste

Directions:

1. Spray the bottom of your frying pan with olive oil or cooking spray.
2. Crack the eggs into the pan. Add salt and pepper as desired. Cook until the whites are firm but the yolk is still runny. Adjust the heat as needed.
3. When ready, flip the eggs over with a spatula and cook for 30 seconds to 1 minute.
4. Remove eggs with a spatula, place them on a plate, and serve with side dishes such as toast, fruit, or breakfast sausages.

Chapter 3: Cooking

Pancakes/Waffle Mix from Scratch

Prep Time: 15 minutes
Makes: 4 large waffles or 12 pancakes

Ingredients:

- 2 eggs
- 2 cups all-purpose flour
- 1¾ cups milk
- ½ cup vegetable oil
- 1 Tbsp. white sugar
- 4 tsp. baking powder
- ¼ tsp. salt
- ½ tsp. vanilla extract

Directions:

1. Preheat the waffle iron.
2. Beat eggs in a large bowl with a hand beater until fluffy.
3. Beat in flour, milk, vegetable oil, sugar, baking powder, salt, and vanilla until smooth.
4. Spray your waffle iron with non-stick cooking spray and allow it to heat.
5. After all ingredients are mixed, pour 1/3 cup mix onto hot waffle iron, pouring into the center to avoid overfilling.
6. Flip over the waffle iron as it cooks. Cook until golden brown and serve immediately.

DRINKS

Orange Smoothie

Ingredients:

- 6 oz. frozen orange juice concentrate
- 1 cup milk
- 1 cup water
- ¼ cup sugar
- 1–2 tsp. vanilla
- 1 cup ice cubes

Directions:

1. Combine all ingredients in the blender.
2. Blend until smooth and serve immediately. Enjoy!

Strawberry Smoothie

Ingredients:

- 1 cup strawberries, sliced (fresh, freeze-dried, or frozen)
- ½ cup milk (nonfat or low-fat)
- ½ cup water
- 1 cup ice
- ¼ cup caster sugar or ¼ cup superfine sugar
- ½–⅔ tsp. vanilla extract

Directions:

1. Slice up fresh strawberries until you have one cup.
2. Add to a blender or food processor.
3. Add the rest of the ingredients.
4. Blend until smooth. You can substitute the water for ice cubes to make a thicker smoothie.
5. Stir in a blender and enjoy!

CHAPTER 3: COOKING

DINNERS AND SIDES

No Yeast Dinner Roll

Ingredients:

- 1 cup flour
- 1 tsp. baking powder
- 1 tsp. salt
- ½ cup milk
- 2 Tbsp. mayo

Directions:

1. Preheat oven to 350°F.
2. Combine all ingredients and spoon into a greased muffin pan.
3. Cook for 15 minutes or until done and golden brown.

Slow Cooker Pork Chops

Prep Time: 5 minutes
Makes: 1–4 servings

Ingredients:

- 1–4 boneless pork chops
- 1 can cream of mushroom soup
- 1 can cream of chicken soup
- 1 packet of onion soup mix
- ½ cup water

Directions:

1. Stir the soups, onion mix, and water in a slow cooker or Crock-Pot. Mix well.
2. Add the pork chops and submerge in sauce.
3. Cover and cook on low for 6–8 hours or on high 4–6 hours. This quick and easy recipe will save you loads of time, and it tastes delicious when paired with mashed potatoes and vegetables.

Spaghetti Sauce from Scratch

Prep Time: 20 minutes
Makes: 6–8 servings

Ingredients:

- 1 (15-ounce) can of diced tomatoes
- 1 (15-ounce) can of tomato sauce
- 1 (6-ounce) can of tomato paste
- 2 Tbsp. sugar (adjust to taste)
- ½ tsp. basil
- ½ tsp. oregano
- ½ tsp. black pepper
- ½ tsp. salt
- 1 tsp. crushed red pepper flakes
- 1 package of mushrooms (optional)

Directions:

1. Throw all ingredients into a saucepan, stir, heat to boiling, then simmer and cover for 20–30 minutes.
2. Season again to taste.
3. Cook some ground beef and chopped onion separately, and boil the spaghetti.
4. Mix, serve, and enjoy!

CHAPTER 3: COOKING

SHRIMP LINGUINE

Prep Time: 30 minutes
Makes: 6–8 servings

Ingredients:

- 6 cloves of garlic (sliced)
- 4 Tbsp. of butter (cubed)
- 1 lemon (for zest)
- 1 lemon (juiced)
- ¼ cup parsley (minced)
- 1–2 lbs shrimp, peeled and deveined
- ½ tsp. baking soda
- 1 tsp. salt
- ¼ tsp. crushed red pepper
- Black pepper, to taste
- 1 (16-oz.) pkg. linguine pasta

Directions:

1. Before cooking, slice the garlic, cube the butter, zest and juice the lemon, and mince the parsley. Put in the fridge until needed.
2. Mix the shrimp, baking soda, salt, red pepper, and black pepper in a mixing bowl. Set aside and let sit for 10 minutes.
3. Boil water for the pasta.
4. Heat a non-stick frying pan for a few minutes, then add olive oil. Add shrimp mix to the pan. Cook for 3 minutes on each side until the shrimp is entirely pink. Once the shrimp is done, move it to a plate and cover it with aluminum foil.
5. Dry off the frying pan, then add olive oil and garlic. Carefully put the pasta in the water to boil, adding 2 tablespoons of kosher salt per gallon of water. If garlic starts to burn, add pasta water as needed. Once the pasta is cooked, start adding it to the pan.
6. Add 4 tablespoons of butter to the pan and stir.
7. Add shrimp mix.
8. If the linguine seems dry, add more pasta water.
9. Add lemon zest and lemon juice.
10. Add parsley and mix everything together.
11. Serve and enjoy. Use leftovers within 1–3 days.

Yorkshire Puddings

Prep Time: 15 minutes
Makes: 12 Puddings

Ingredients:

- 1 tsp. oil or dripping
- 1 cup plain flour
- 4 eggs
- 1 cup milk
- Salt to taste
- Rosemary and sage (if desired)

Directions:

1. Preheat the oven to 425°F (220°C).
2. Put oil or dripping in each of several muffin tins, or a couple of tablespoons in a larger roasting tin, and place in the oven until the fat is hot and beginning to smoke (about 7 minutes).
3. Combine the flour, eggs, milk, and salt and beat to form a thick batter.
4. Add the herbs of your choice if you wish.
5. When the fat begins to smoke, take the tin out of the oven and place it over a low light so that it doesn't cool.
6. Pour in the batter. If you're using muffin tins, don't overfill. Use a ¼ cup measuring cup per tin to make it even, then distribute the rest evenly. Take care—it will be hot.
7. Make sure there is space in your oven; the puddings will rise as they cook.
8. Put the tin back into the oven and cook for about 30–45 minutes, by which time they will be puffed and crisp. Serve with gravy and the roast dinner of your choice.

CHAPTER 3: COOKING

Egg Salad

Prep Time: 25 mins
Makes: 4 servings

Ingredients:

- 6 large eggs
- ¼ cup mayonnaise
- 1 Tbsp. mustard
- Salt and pepper

Directions:

1. Place eggs in a pot of water.
2. Bring the water to a boil, remove it from the heat, and let the eggs sit in the hot water for 15 minutes.
3. Remove eggs from hot water. Run cool water into the pan, drain, and refrigerate until cool.
4. Peel the cooled eggs and dice or mash them.
5. Mix the mayonnaise and mustard, then combine with the eggs.
6. Add salt and pepper to taste.
7. Refrigerate for at least an hour.

DEVILED EGGS

Prep Time: 15–20 minutes
Makes: 18 deviled eggs

Ingredients:

- 18 eggs, boiled, peeled, halved
- ½ cup mayo
- 2 Tbsp. spicy brown mustard
- 4–5 strips of bacon
- ¼ tsp. paprika

Directions:

1. Mix together the egg yolks, mayo, and spicy brown mustard, and scoop the mixture into each egg half.
2. Cut 4–5 strips of bacon into 1/4-inch pieces.
3. Sprinkle paprika onto each deviled egg and insert a piece of bacon in the center.
4. Serve and enjoy.

Whole Wheat Bread

Prep Time: 45 minutes
Makes: 5 loaves

Ingredients:

- 5½–6 cups very warm water
- ½ cup of honey or sugar
- 3 Tbsp. dry yeast
- 1½ Tbsp. salt
- ⅓–½ cup dry milk powder (optional)
- 2–4 Tbsp. dough enhancer (optional)
- 2 Tbsp. Gluten (optional)
- ½ cup vegetable oil
- 12–16 cups whole wheat flour

Directions:

1. Add water, sugar or honey, yeast, salt, dry milk, dough enhancer, and gluten. Mix. Add oil and then slowly add flour 1 cup at a time. You will have enough flour when the dough pulls away from the mixer. Let the mixer continue to knead the dough for ten minutes.
2. Empty the mixer onto a greased surface. Divide into 5 equal pieces (use a kitchen scale if needed). Mold the dough into loaves and put them into a greased bread pan.
3. Put the dough on top of your oven and preheat the oven to 400°F. Let rise for 10–15 minutes under a clean damp cloth.
4. Bake at 400°F for 6 minutes. Then bake at 350°F for 25–30 minutes.
5. Cool before cutting the loaf.

MEAL PLANNER

Monday
Breakfast :
Lunch :
Dinner :

Tuesday
Breakfast :
Lunch :
Dinner :

Wednesday
Breakfast :
Lunch :
Dinner :

Thursday
Breakfast :
Lunch :
Dinner :

Friday
Breakfast :
Lunch :
Dinner :

Saturday
Breakfast :
Lunch :
Dinner :

Sunday
Breakfast :
Lunch :
Dinner :

Shopping List

4
Health Care

"Do what you can, with what you have, where you are."

—Theodore Roosevelt [6]

If you don't have your health, you don't have anything.

Just as we count on good doctors and facilities to visit when we need treatment for our illnesses, our bodies count on us to make good decisions and take care of them. You are the custodian of your body. You're responsible for what you put into it and ultimately what you get out of it.

On Taking Care of Yourself

Your life is your movie. It's up to you to adapt to changes and sustain your health. You're responsible for improving and flourishing in whatever existence you carve out for yourself. Whether you have a positive or negative mental outlook makes all the difference in your success and overall happiness.

Treat yourself well, keep your living space clean and bright, and take care of your mental and physical health. Make decisions that will benefit you in the long run and make your future self proud to look back on. Adopt healthy life habits and routines that will benefit you.

Health Records and Medical History

Ensure you have access to your health insurance information, immunization history, and contact information when visiting health care providers or having routine checkups. If you have a medical condition, keep a file of your discharge papers, records, and receipts and be prepared to access your information. Keep track of any vaccination or shot information you might need to show when you head to specific job interviews or doctor consultations.

Checking Your Blood Pressure

When we're young, we feel invincible. We eat what we want and have superhuman metabolism and endless energy. Nothing can faze us. But the truth is, the higher a person's blood pressure, the greater their risk of health problems. If high blood pressure is left untreated, it can lead to stroke, heart attack, kidney failure, and heart failure. Checking your blood pressure can help you gauge where you stand health-wise and pinpoint any medical treatment or preventative care needed.

You can do a few things if you suspect you have high blood pressure. Doctor's offices can take your blood pressure at appointments. Most clinics will let you come in to get your blood pressure checked regularly without a charge. There are also free blood pressure machines at Walmart, Kroger, and CVS pharmacies. Take a minute to relax, sit, and check your blood pressure. If it is abnormal or high, consult a doctor.

Premature Aging

Certain lifestyle choices—such as smoking, drinking, dehydration, and lack of sleep—accelerate the aging process, causing fine lines, wrinkles, and unhealthy skin. Premature aging can be prevented and treated by proper skin care, regular exercise, good sleeping habits, and drinking lots of water. Protect your skin by wearing sunscreen and hats.

On Self-Care

Self-care is vital for everyone. As you navigate the challenges of adulthood, take care of your physical and mental health. Prioritize your well-being so you feel capable and healthy.

Regardless of age, overall health care is essential to improve your chances of living a long and healthy life. Invest in yourself, whether you take classes to improve specific skills or invest in a healthier lifestyle. Investments pay off in the long run. Step out of your comfort zone and reach out for help when needed.

Here are some self-care tips to help you take better care of yourself:

- Be patient. Healthy self-care habits take time to develop. Don't get discouraged if you slip up—just keep trying. Eventually, you'll find what works for you.
- If you struggle to care for yourself, don't hesitate to ask for help from friends, family, or a therapist.
- Spend time in nature. Get fresh air and sunshine to help you relax and de-stress.
- Meditation and yoga are great ways to reduce stress and improve mental focus.
- Read a book or listen to music to help you relax and escape everyday stresses.
- Set aside time for loved ones. Take the time to show loved ones you care about them, and you will feel supported and valued.
- Find a support system. A group of people who support you can make a big difference in your self-care journey.
- Whether you like to read, play a sport, or walk, do an activity you enjoy daily.

Self-care is a process you must work for, but the payoff is worth it. Self-care improves physical and mental health, reduces stress, and boosts mood. So make self-care the first order of business and take better care of yourself today.

Visits to the Doctor

Schedule an appointment with a doctor and dentist twice a year for cleanings and check-ups. If you're a woman, select a reputable OB-GYN and get regular pap smears. In addition to exercising and maintaining a healthy diet, taking care of your health will elongate your lifespan and pinpoint any possible problems early on.

If you suspect something is wrong, you've gained weight, you feel lethargic, or you are low in energy, visit your doctor and ask them to take a blood test. Blood tests are excellent for finding irregularities in our systems, such as thyroid issues, diabetes, the onset of cancer, and infections. Preventative treatment makes all the difference in your future health.

Find a Primary Care Provider

A primary care provider (PCP) is the doctor you should see for routine checkups and any minor health problems. Find the right doctor for you to promote a lifetime of good health.

There are multiple ways to find the right PCP. Word of mouth is a popular method. Inquire about doctors that family, friends, neighbors, and coworkers like. Firsthand accounts of people's experiences with different doctors are priceless. Check with your insurance company to find an in-network doctor. Many insurance companies have websites or apps that make this more convenient.

Look online. Schedule an appointment once you've located a doctor you want to see. An initial visit will allow you to meet the doctor and see if they suit you well.

When you choose a PCP, consider the following factors:

CHAPTER 4: HEALTH CARE

- **Location.** Find a doctor in a nearby, convenient location.
- **Insurance.** Make sure the doctor accepts your insurance.
- **Availability.** Some doctors have longer appointment wait times than others.
- **Specialties.** If you have specific health conditions, find a doctor who specializes in those areas.
- **Personality.** Find a doctor you trust and feel comfortable with.

Once you've selected a PCP, build a relationship with your doctor. The more you know your doctor, the more at ease you'll feel when you talk to them. Don't be afraid to advocate for yourself. If you're unhappy with the care you receive, don't hesitate to speak up. You have the right to get proper care.

To make the initial visit easier, have your health history written down or typed on your phone to make the office paperwork more manageable. Be prepared to answer medical questions. Ask questions about the doctor's experience and approach to health care. Trust your gut. If you're unsatisfied, looking for service elsewhere is okay.

Your Overall Health

There are three parts of your body you should always take care of as you age:

1. Your mouth and teeth. Practice good oral hygiene. Brush your teeth twice a day and use dental floss and mouthwash. Visit your dentist for biannual cleanings.
2. Your feet and nails. The overall health of your feet can affect the rest of your body. Keep your fingernails and toenails trimmed, scrub beneath your nails when you wash your hands, and treat your feet to vinegar-solution foot baths and pedicures.
3. Your eyes. Get regular eye exams and take breaks from computer and phone screens to rest your eyes. Have one day of the week when you strive to limit your technology use as much as possible.

Preventing Diabetes

Over 29 million Americans have diabetes. As you age, weight loss gets trickier, and you become more susceptible to diseases and illnesses. To reduce the risk of diabetes, you can do the following:

- **Lose ten pounds**. Every kilogram of weight loss (approximately 2.2 pounds) reduces your risk of diabetes by 16 percent. If you're overweight, start a healthy diet and you'll feel better with each pound lost.
- **Cut your sugar intake by half**. Use a raw or organic sugar substitute to lower sugar consumption. Use honey in your tea instead of sugar, and avoid sugary foods. Always ask for the sugar-free option. Buy low- or no-cholesterol foods and light margarine instead of butter.
- **Exercise and drink water**. Going to the gym is a game-changer. Our bodies need water, and they respond well to exercise. Moving our bodies improves circulation and sharpens mental agility. Find time to get up and moving every day, regardless of how long.

  Move around from the second you wake up. Stretch your body. Take the stairs instead of the elevator at work. Do those chores, go for a walk, swim a few laps, do yoga, ride a bike, or find a fun physical activity you love. Physical inactivity increases the likelihood of diabetes. Walking is a healthy way to combat the risk. Drink plenty of water. Hydrating replenishes your skin, keeps you healthy, and gives you energy. Being dehydrated can shrink your brain cells. People may joke about getting brain fog, but that might be exactly what they have because they aren't getting enough water.
- **Get sleep**. Set a bedtime and stick to it. Get 7–9 hours of sleep a night. You'll not only fight the risk of obesity and diabetes, but you'll also feel more energetic and productive at work and school.

Diarrhea and BRAT

Suppose you or anyone in the home gets diarrhea. In that case, over-the-counter medicines help, but always remember the BRAT diet (bananas, rice, applesauce, toast). These cost-effective and overlooked foods will help get rid of diarrhea. If you get diarrhea, have some crisp toast, a ripe banana, some applesauce, or a bowl of steamed rice with soy sauce. Remember to drink water, eat lots of fiber, and replenish your fluids.

First Aid

For superficial cuts, apply pressure with a clean cloth or bandage. Once the bleeding has stopped, clean the wound, dress it with antibiotic ointment or spray, and help keep the wound clean by changing the Band-Aid or fabric every two hours. Always keep an ice pack in the freezer in case of bumps or bruises.

Check Your Urine and Stools

Get into the habit of glancing at your pee and poop color. Yep, you read that correctly. Before you flush, check the color of your urine. The lighter the color, the healthier and more hydrated you are. Checking your urine can also help detect early signs of bladder or kidney trouble. See a doctor if you notice blood in your urine or stool and you're not menstruating.

Stress Management

Moving out and being on your own is a big deal.

It's a transition that is, by itself, a significant milestone. Add to that the engulfing stress of starting a job, finding an apartment or home, and going to college, and you have one potent stress salad. If you're feeling overwhelmed, try the following:

1. **Prioritize.** Adopt a working schedule with your routines. Being organized and having an action plan for your daily tasks and activities brings a sense of order and comfort. Make to-do lists and write things down to prioritize better. Group your stressors into two categories: those you have control over and those you

don't. Make changes to the things you can control, and endeavor to stop stressing over those you can't.

2. **Personalize your workspace.** Put up a photo, an inspirational quote, or something that helps you relax and motivates your ambitions.

3. **Avoid distractions.** Turn the phone on vibrate, put it away, close the social media windows, and focus on what you're doing. In today's society, we have technology and entertainment at our fingertips. Still, if we don't put them away occasionally, they can overwhelm our already busy lives. Focus on your job, your relationships, and what's important.

4. **Make your life fun!** Take brain breaks. Have a calendar or a joke app that makes you laugh. If you're a dancing cat person, watch that video on a loop once in a while and laugh your head off. Enjoy your life and take a few minutes out of each day to have fun with it.

5. **Adopt calming techniques.** Try yoga or meditation. There are great mindfulness apps for phones, many of which are free. Find one that works for you. Go for a calm walk around your school or workplace during lunch and feel the sun on your face. Once you feel centered and can relax, you'll feel less stressed.

6. **Check out fidget toys such as spinners, stress balls, and cubes.** Guess what? They're not just for kids. If you can't sit still or need to keep your fingers busy, put a fidget cube in your pants pocket or spin a fidget spinner whenever necessary. Keep them out of meetings and classes, though, because they can be distracting.

7. **Sleep well and eat right.** While there's a lot to get done, the first thing you need to worry about is your health. Go to bed early to get that extra hour of sleep. Eat right and take care of your body—after all, it's your only one. Be mindful of your overall health; what you do with it is up to you.

8. **Exercise.** Get exercise at least three times a week and find a physical activity you enjoy.

9. **Spend time on personal care.** Get that haircut, makeover, or facial you've been wanting. Treat yourself to a mani-pedi or relax in a bubble bath. You work hard. You deserve it.

10. **Go out with friends or have them over for dinner.** Socializing is essential, and we need friends. Nurture meaningful and

Chapter 4: Health Care

positive social connections with others. Spend time with people who uplift you and believe in you. Do random acts of kindness and cherish your friendships.

SELF-CARE
Checklist

	M	T	W	TH	F	SA	SU
Drink a glass of water to start the day	☐	☐	☐	☐	☐	☐	☐
Enjoy 45 minutes of exercise	☐	☐	☐	☐	☐	☐	☐
Get some fresh air	☐	☐	☐	☐	☐	☐	☐
Have a healthy breakfast	☐	☐	☐	☐	☐	☐	☐
Enjoy a warm morning drink	☐	☐	☐	☐	☐	☐	☐
Plan out your day in your planner	☐	☐	☐	☐	☐	☐	☐
Stretch your body	☐	☐	☐	☐	☐	☐	☐
Take regular breaks	☐	☐	☐	☐	☐	☐	☐
Enjoy some sunshine	☐	☐	☐	☐	☐	☐	☐
Take hot/cold bath or shower	☐	☐	☐	☐	☐	☐	☐
Read something meaningful	☐	☐	☐	☐	☐	☐	☐
Play some invigorating music	☐	☐	☐	☐	☐	☐	☐
Disconnect	☐	☐	☐	☐	☐	☐	☐
Eat a healthy snack	☐	☐	☐	☐	☐	☐	☐
Wind down by avoiding bright light at night	☐	☐	☐	☐	☐	☐	☐
Get in bed before 10pm	☐	☐	☐	☐	☐	☐	☐

5

Everyday Hacks

"Do the difficult things while they are easy and do the great things while they are small. A journey of a thousand miles must begin with a single step."

—Lao Tzu [7]

TAKING THE EASY WAY OUT MAY GET A BAD RAP THESE DAYS, BUT LET'S face it—there are times when it's super helpful to cut cleaning corners. There's nothing wrong with chopping time and money in half to make your life more efficient. Here are some everyday hacks for you to use and enjoy.

How to Get Rid of Hiccups

1. Fill your lungs with your mouth and hold your breath.
2. Swallow three times in a row.
3. Exhale slowly through your nostrils.

If the hiccups are still there, try downing a glass of water.

Smelly Garbage Disposal?

Eat an orange, rip the peel into little pieces, and put the peel in the garbage disposal. Run hot water, turn on the disposal, and let it work for thirty seconds. It will get rid of the smell.

Use Bread to Pick Up Broken Glass Shards

Press a slice of bread over the smaller shards (after picking up the larger ones), and it should come off. Immediately throw the bread in the trash and sweep the area.

Smelly Shoes?

Place a dryer sheet in each shoe overnight. In the morning, it will smell fresh as new. Alternatively, place a few dry tea bags inside each shoe.

Body Odor?

If you find yourself in a situation without deodorant and smelling unsightly, cut an orange into two halves and rub the orange onto your skin. The natural deodorant will eliminate any smell.

Clean an Icky Microwave in Five Minutes

Mix 1/3 cup vinegar with 1 cup water in a bowl and microwave uncovered for five minutes. As soon as the time is up, it should wipe clean with a damp disposable sponge. For the more challenging areas, dip a sponge corner into the vinegar solution (be careful not to burn yourself) and cleanse the dirty areas. The vinegar steam cleans the microwave and is a natural disinfectant with no ammonia. Dry the microwave with a clean paper towel. Wash the glass turnstile with soapy dishwater, rinse, and dry before replacing it. Clean off the soapy residue before finishing.

Helpful Hint: Clean out your microwave once a month. Keeping it clean will increase its lifespan.

Sanitize Your Sponges

Change your dish sponges weekly. To prolong the life of a sponge, wash it with warm tap water, wring it out, and heat it in the microwave for two minutes. Steaming the sponge in the microwave will eliminate bacteria and re-puff it to its usual size. This method is also suitable if you want to recycle and sanitize an old sponge for cleaning the bathroom.

Protect Stove Top Burners

If you have an electric stove or live in an apartment, cover the stove top burner pans (the silver round things beneath the burners) with aluminum foil to preserve the cleanliness of the stove top. Stove top burner pans on electric stoves can get burnt out and icky. Cover them with aluminum foil, and you can change them when it collects grease and grime. Protecting the burners will save you time and money, as the stove will be good as new when you move out.

Water Spill or Pipe Leak?

Cat litter is absorbent. If your pipes leak or you sustain water flooding damages, pour down some cat litter to absorb the water.

Uncontrollable Coughing?

Raise your hands above your head to make it stop.

Do You Have a Migraine?

Drink some grape juice.

Are You Having Chafing Problems?

Rub deodorant between your thighs.

Static Problem?

Attach a safety pin to whatever piece of clothing is causing the static, and it will stop.

Rust?

Soak a square piece of aluminum foil in white vinegar and rub it on the rust. This mixture will remove the rust.

Grimy, Icky Stove Top

Mix a 1:1 ratio of hydrogen peroxide and baking soda in a plastic bowl with a disposable plastic spoon. Mix until you have a good, thick paste. Spread over a crusty or icky stove top, and let it sit for a few minutes. Scrub with a disposable old sponge, washing and rinsing the sponge each time you wipe to get it sterile. Make sure you wear dishwashing gloves for this.

You may have to do it twice for grimy, greasy stove tops, but it works like a charm, and you can clean it in five to ten minutes with minimal hassle. It's also toxin-free and better for the environment. To clean the oven burner brackets for gas stoves, set them in warm dishwashing water and scrub them with a scouring or scrubbing sponge. Most grime will come off if you let it soak for a few minutes beforehand.

To Keep Water on the Stove from Boiling Over

Put a wooden spoon across the top of the pot.

Are Weeds Growing in the Sidewalk Cracks?

Pour boiling water over them. Boiling water is a chemical-free solution. The weeds will become brittle, breakable, and easy to pull from the root up.

Clean Your Dishwasher and Washing Machine with Vinegar

Vinegar is naturally acidic and will sterilize your dishwasher and laundry washer. Scrub out your dishwasher, fill a measuring cup with 1 cup of white vinegar, place the vinegar-filled measuring cup inside the dishwasher, and run a single dishwashing cycle all on its own. The vinegar steam cleans everything and sterilizes it. You can do the same for your washer: pour in one cup of vinegar and run a wash cycle. It prolongs the life of the equipment, and you'll notice the difference immediately. Check beforehand that both appliances are vinegar-safe.

To Remove Hard Water Stains from a Metal Faucet or Backsplash

Slice a lemon in half and rub vigorously on the hard water stains. Let it sit for five minutes, then clean it with warm water and a sponge. It should remove a considerable amount of the hard water stains and shine it up. Repeat for harder-to-remove stains as many times as needed.

To Clean Grimy Shower Heads

Pour white vinegar into a plastic shopping bag or freezer bag and secure it to the head with a rubber band. Either leave it overnight or run the shower for a minute, effectively cleaning it.

To Clean a Toilet Brush

After rinsing the toilet brush out, wedge the handle between the toilet seat lid and the toilet, allowing it to drip-dry into the toilet for an hour or two if possible. Pour a capful of Pine-Sol or scented floor cleaner into the toilet brush base to sanitize between uses, and clean the bottom out once a month with soap and water.

Running Low on Tube Stuff?

If you're running low on hair gel or about to finish a beauty product in a tube, cut the tube in half. Dig out the leftover product with a Q-tip, use it, and seal the remnants with a sandwich bag until you've used it all.

Wrinkly Shirt But No Iron?

Hang it in the bathroom on a towel rack, and then take a shower. The steam from your shower or bath will naturally steam the wrinkles out. Alternatively, you can throw your wrinkled shirt or outfit in the dryer with a wet sock for thirty minutes.

Lost an Earring in the Carpet?

Cover a vacuum cleaner hose with nylon or pantyhose. Secure a rubber band over it, turn on the vacuum, and search the area. You should be able to find and salvage the jewelry without it getting sucked into the void.

To Get Rid of Fruit Flies

Fill a bowl with a 1:1 ratio of apple cider vinegar and dish soap, then leave it out. Fruit flies are attracted to the vinegar, and the soap will kill them.

CHAPTER 5: EVERYDAY HACKS

To Better Organize Your Freezer

Use black paper clip clamps to hang frozen vegetables below a shelf rack. This will clear up space.

Heating Leftovers

To heat food better in a microwave, make a circle in the middle of the food (like a donut), leaving a space.

Slice Cheese and Cakes

Use unscented dental floss for a perfect slice.

Freeze and Store Eggs

Crack eggs and lightly scramble until the yolk and whites are blended. Add one teaspoon of salt or sugar per cup to help the freezing process so the eggs' gelatinous property doesn't thicken during the freezing process. You can also separate the whites if you only eat the protein. If you use individual eggs, shorten the seasoning to an eighth of a teaspoon per egg and put it into individual ice cube trays. Thaw as needed and transfer to freezer bags. Frozen eggs, when stored properly, will last up to a year.

Freeze a 16–20 oz. Bottle of Water Overnight

Use a frozen water bottle as an ice pack for your work or school lunch if you're out of ice packs.

Instantly Chill a Drink without Ice Cubes

Take a plastic bottle of your desired drink at room temperature, wrap a wet paper towel around it, and put it in the freezer. It will be ice-cold in fifteen minutes.

Need More Counter Space?

Pull out a top drawer and place your cutting board over it.

Mount Your iPad or Handheld Device

Mount it anywhere by using plastic adhesive hooks from the dollar store.

Loose Zipper That Keeps Opening on Jeans or Coats?

Find an old key ring and attach it to the end of your zipper head, zip up your jeans/coat, and then attach the ring around your jeans/coat button. Fashioning this makeshift zipper will keep the zipper in place and is still detachable for bathroom breaks and changing until you buy a new pair of jeans.

Stuck Zipper?

Use a No. 2 pencil and WD-40 (or cooking spray) to lightly coat the teeth of the zipper, which should be more pliant. Check the zipper's individual teeth to ensure they're all straight. Use pliers to straighten if needed.

Zipper Head Broke or Fell Off

Use a paperclip, cord, or an old key ring. Loop it through the hole by the base of the zipper and it should work.

Are Your Jeans Too Tight?

Loop something elastic, like a rubber band, through the buttonhole on your jeans, tie it securely, and then loop the loose end around the button. This will give you a few more inches of baby room or comfort.

> *Helpful Hint:* You'll need to wear a loose, long top to cover the button, but the jeans will be more comfortable. Invest in stretchable maternity clothes if you're pregnant.

Use a Bobby Pin

Use bobby pins to keep a chip bag clipped shut, clean up the edges of nails, or mine out the last bit of toothpaste. You can also tape one onto a roll of clear tape so you don't lose the end. Paper clips also work well for this.

To Stay Cool When the Power Is Out

During a heat wave, hang wet sheets over doorways. Hot air will cool as it passes through the damp fabric. Use cooling towels and handheld fans to stay cool. Go to the lowest level of your building and use blackout curtains on the windows to reflect the heat. If you use aluminum foil on the windows, remember to place it with the shiny side facing out and cover the backside with something insulating like cardboard. Stay hydrated to beat the heat.

Take Uber and Lyft

Look into Uber and Lyft if you don't have a car. They are cheaper than taxis, and you can split the costs with your friends if you ride together. If you're picky about your particular ride, Uber has a nicer selection of vehicles.

Collect Your Pennies and Loose Change

There are Coinstar machines in major grocery stores, and you can amass a reasonably large amount if you chuck change into an old jar or piggy bank. Coinstar will allow you to cash the money, donate it, or use it for in-store purchases.

Meditate

Meditating lowers your blood pressure and targets your clarity and stress management. Take at least five minutes a day to close your eyes and focus on where you see yourself in the future.

Sleep on Your Back

When you sleep on your back, your weight evenly distributes, and many experts have found that it also helps prevent wrinkles.

Repainting

Colors can affect your mood, and a color change can make all the difference. If a room feels oppressive or dark, repaint the walls a lighter, neutral color (if your apartment or home allows this). Read up on Feng Shui and move items around to have a more spacious, positive feel.

Need an Ice Pack?

Saturate a sponge, seal it in a sandwich bag, and freeze it overnight for an ice pack that won't leak. Throw it in your work lunch box for a lighter-weight ice pack.

Run Out of Eyeliner? Use Eyeshadow

1. Get two or three clean Q-tips (or cotton buds), some old or used dark eyeshadow, and mascara.
2. Run the tip of one Q-tip beneath lukewarm water. Be sure to soak it well.
3. Apply the tip-top point of the wet Q-tip to the desired shade. Circle it around, accumulating a small dot of color on the Q-tip.
4. Apply the eyeshadow to your eyes the same as you would eyeliner—the smaller the dot on the Q-tip, the cleaner the makeup. Line the top of your eyes, then finish with mascara.

Lose the Back of an Earring?

Snip a small, slivered portion off the end of a pencil eraser, and it will hold the earring in place.

Have a Small Run in Your Pantyhose?

Coat the edges of the tear with clear nail polish to avoid it spreading to the rest of the pantyhose until you can get new ones.

Have Paint on Your Clothes?

Use a razor to remove it.

Eye Contact

Looking into people's eyes during conversations will help them like you more and establish trust.

Shop at Farmers' Markets

Farmers' markets offer freshly picked produce at cost-effective prices. You will get more bang for your buck.

Want to Eat Out But Don't Have Cash?

If you like to dine out with friends but are low on funds, have a meal beforehand and order the salad bar or a soup and salad for five or ten dollars.

Out of Cup Holders?

Use a shoe! Shoe cup holders work well at tailgates and picnics and in cars.

Dirty Sneakers?

Use an old toothbrush and toothpaste and go to town to remove dirt. The toothbrush method also restores old sneakers.

Cut Sponges in Half

This will save both money and overuse.

Clean Dust

Use old socks to clean dusty surfaces.

Impromptu Chip Clip

Use a broken plastic pants hanger (just the clip portion) as a clip for bags of chips, crackers, or cereal. Recycle the remnants in a nearby plastic recycle bin.

Clean Car Headlights

Use toothpaste to clean a cloudy car headlight.

Keep Food Warm on the Road

Use your passenger car seat warmer to keep a potluck dish or pizza hot while driving.

Maximize a Small Living Space

Put your whiteboard on your coffee table to save wall space. You can write things down, doodle, or organize your thoughts as you watch TV. If your coffee table has an alcove beneath it, you can store your whiteboard there when not in use. Use fold-out desks, tall shelves, and closets for space-saving options.

SELF-CARE HACKS

- ✓ **Begin each day with a positive affirmation**
  Set a positive tone for your day by starting each morning with intent. Remind yourself about your goals and envision your successful day.

- ✓ **Practise mindfulness or meditation**
  Take a few minutes to get centered through mindfulness/meditation. This will reduce stress, improve your focus, and promote good health.

- ✓ **Make physical activity a priority**
  Do at least ONE physical activity each day. Exercise releases endorphins, boosts your energy, and improves mental health.

- ✓ **Unplug and walk away**
  Disconnecting from technology reduces the stress we put on our eyes and minds. Taking regular screen breaks will improve your sleep quality, help you focus better, and be more productive.

- ✓ **Eat healthy**
  Nourish your body with a balanced, healthy diet rich in fruits, vegetables, whole grains, and proteins. Stay hydrated and keep drinking water.

- ✓ **Get enough rest**
  Endeavor to sleep at least 7-9 hours each night. Practice good sleep hygiene and create a calming routine that helps you rest.

- ✓ **Pick up a hobby**
  Make time for pursuits you enjoy that stir you creatively. Hobbies help you express yourself and reduce stress.

- ✓ **Reach out to loved ones**
  Nurture your relationships with others by reaching out to them on a regular basis. Social connections promote your overall well being.

- ✓ **Stay thankful**
  Practise gratitude and reflect on what you are thankful for in a journal.

- ✓ **Set healthy boundaries**
  Prioritize your self-care by setting boundaries and learning to say no when it's necessary, in both your personal and professional life.

6

Home Remedies

"Nature itself is the best physician."

—Hippocrates [8]

Honey, lemon, garden-grown herbs, and essential oils. What do these have in common? They are all simple yet powerful ingredients you can find and use in your home. Thousands of years ago, the ancient Chinese and Egyptians used home remedies in healing rituals and religious ceremonies. Their natural use still rings true and carries on today. Here are some helpful home remedies.

Treating Dandruff

Add tea tree oil to your shampoo or conditioner to help prevent dandruff and itchiness. Add a cap of white vinegar to each load of laundry for a week to help rid the clothes of dandruff. If your dandruff worsens, seek a dandruff-treatment shampoo and consult a doctor.

Trouble Sleeping?

- Establish a bedtime. Try to develop a habit of going to bed on time each night. Our bodies respond well to routines.
- Exercise at least three or four times a week. Proper exercise will help with a good night's rest, and it can also alleviate stress.
- Take a warm bath.
- Have a drink of warm, steamed milk with nutmeg or cinnamon.
- Avoid caffeinated drinks after midday because they can increase nighttime urination.
- Avoid large meals late at night.
- Try to meditate or listen to relaxing music.
- Turn off all electronic devices and technology two hours before bedtime for better rest.
- Spend as much time as possible outdoors in the morning light. Go for an outdoor walk on your lunch break.

Drink Cucumber Water

Drinking cucumber water can help clear up your skin. Slice up cucumbers (they're cheap), put them in a pitcher with filtered water, and let them soak overnight. Cucumber water has many health benefits (including aiding in tissue and muscle health), is low in calories, and is good for skin care and detoxifying. Plus it's affordable.

Having Fun with Essential Oils

- **Lip Balm:** For softening lip balm with a bit of zing, melt 2 oz. (50 g) of sweet almond oil with 1/4 oz. (7 g) of beeswax in a double boiler. Remove from heat and stir in 1 teaspoon of organic set honey. Whizz into a cream with an electric whisk and add a few drops of lemon or peppermint essential oil. Pour into an old lip balm pot or miniature screw-top jam jar and set in the fridge. The lip balm will keep for about 6 months if stored correctly.
- **Face Mask/Pack:** For a nourishing, moisturizing face pack that smells nice and is suitable for dry skin, mash a ripe banana with

2 tablespoons of sweet almond oil and a fresh organic egg yolk. Smear on your face, leaving for up to 10 minutes. Rinse off with warm water.

- **Exfoliant / Body Scrub:** Make a micro-beaded exfoliant. Mix 1 tablespoon of sea salt (grind with a pestle and mortar to make them more micro), 1 tablespoon of honey, and 2 tablespoons of olive oil. You can use it in the bath on both your face and body. It's cheap and smells nice while being toxin-free. It's easier if stored in a small pot or jar.
- **Body Talc:** Make your own deliciously scented talc by adding 20 drops of mandarin essential oil and 10 drops of orange essential oil to 6 tablespoons of cornstarch. You can store this in an old talcum powder dispenser, which will keep for up to 6 months.
- **Perfume:** Make a toxin-free cologne by adding 18 drops of your favorite essential oil to 2 tablespoons vodka. Sandalwood and rose oil make lovely perfumes for women.

Grape-Seed Oil

Grape-seed oil will last three times as long as any store-bought anti-aging skin cream. After washing your face at night and once in the morning, dab a dime-sized amount of grapeseed oil under each eye. It works as a skin toner in addition to fighting wrinkles, and it does the same thing as an anti-aging eye cream but without using whale oil components.

Grape-seed oil is also great for your hair because it contains many essential minerals. It promotes healthy hair growth and doubles as an organic dandruff treatment. You can pat a small amount on your hair a few times a week—better if done after a shower when your hair's still damp.

Sunburns

Pure aloe vera is the most extraordinary natural remedy for sunburns. Aloe vera has proven to promote healing and is the best way to soothe sore skin. Look for pure aloe vera gel (over 97 percent aloe content) in your local health food store or the grocery store's first aid aisle.

Air Freshener

Mix one teaspoon of your favorite essential oil with 250 ml (8 fl. oz.) water. Store in a spray bottle and spray two or three times in the center of the room.

Lemon Juice

Lemon juice is a natural bleach and fabric whitener, effective deodorizer, degreaser, and disinfectant. As a substitute for baking soda, slice a lemon in half, sprinkle salt on it, and put it facing up in your fridge door for two to three days—it gets rid of odors. Lemon juice will also clean and lighten the wood on a cutting board.

Honey

Honey is liquid gold used throughout centuries by kings and queens in Egypt and elsewhere. They don't call it the nectar of the gods for nothing! Honey is not only delicious with an indefinite shelf life, but it also has anti-bacterial properties and helps reduce inflammatory issues. Substituting sugar for honey helps promote weight loss and is healthier for your body.

Use honey in tea for a sore throat, as a face wash, to soothe chapped lips, to treat acne and mosquito bites, or to help relieve a cough. Make a delicious, affordable, and nutritious peanut butter and honey sandwich, or add one teaspoon honey to a half cup warm milk for an organic hair mask. The possibilities and benefits are endless!

White Distilled Vinegar

White vinegar is acidic, which can neutralize alkaline substances like limescale. It's also an effective disinfectant, antifungal agent, and degreaser. It's suitable to use on bathroom sinks and toilets and a great alternative to bleach.

Here are some essential oils you can use without diluting to promote wellness:

- **Lavender oil** can be used in everything. It is de-stressing, it can be worn as a perfume, and you can put a few drops in the bath to relax. It also is excellent when added to the final cycle when washing clothes.
- **Neroli oil** is mood-enhancing. It's great to add a few drops into the bath for kids to help moisturize, and it makes any plain massage oil smell wonderful.
- **Rose oil** is great as a facial cream. Add two drops of evening primrose oil for a great facial oil before bed.
- **Bergamot oil** soothes itchy scalps and skin. A few drops added to your shampoo or conditioner help if you have itchy or dry skin. It's also useful after camping.
- **Frankincense oil** helps prevent wrinkles. Mix frankincense with lavender oil and add it to hand cream or a natural body lotion for a pleasant scent—about a 1:1 ratio when mixing.

Get a Plant

Buy a plant. It doesn't matter if it's a cactus, bamboo plant, ivy, or yucca. Alternatively, you can get dried eucalyptus branches to give your living room a bit of aromatherapy. But have one living thing in your house that you can take care of, nurture, and watch as it grows. Plants thwart depression, increase oxygen in the air, and make you feel better.

Become Proficient at Reading Ingredients

Read the ingredients when you buy shampoo, conditioner, makeup, or any household or hygiene product. Avoid ones that have fragrance (*parfum*) or cocamidopropyl betaine in them.

Homemade Jewelry Cleaner

Ingredients:

- 1 Tbsp. salt
- 1 Tbsp. baking soda
- 1 Tbsp. dish detergent
- 1 cup water
- 1 square of aluminum foil

Directions:

1. Heat water in the microwave for 1–2 minutes.
2. Cut a square of aluminum foil and cover the bottom of a small bowl (like a cereal bowl or Tupperware container).
3. Pour hot water into the bowl. Combine salt, soda, and dishwashing liquid in the bowl. Place the jewelry on the foil and let it sit for 5–10 minutes. Rinse the jewelry in cool water and dry it with a soft cloth. Discard the solution after use and make a new batch next time.
4. This mix works well for gold-filled brass, German (nickel) silver, and sterling silver. It can also clean jewelry with freshwater pearls, shell cameos, and mother of pearls.

Home Remedy Tips

While home remedies are never a substitute for medical treatment, they come in handy and allow you to help the environment.

Please note that if you experience severe symptoms, always consult a doctor.

CHAPTER 6: HOME REMEDIES

Try the different home remedy tips below for a greener, happier lifestyle.

- Rake coffee grounds in the soil to fertilize plants and keep them vigorous and robust.
- Add eggshells to the soil to improve plant nutrition and growth.
- Grind citrus peels and sprinkle them on plants to repel pests and boost nutrition.
- Place an open box of baking soda in the fridge to deodorize and soak up foul odors.
- Place a water bottle upside down in the soil to drip water plants when you're away.
- Use a humidifier to relieve congestion and help you breathe better.
- Eat chicken soup. Chicken soup has anti-inflammatory properties and relieves cold and flu symptoms.
- To relieve pain and inflammation, drape a hot water bottle or heating pad over the affected area.
- Sprinkle 1–2 cups of Epsom salt into a warm bath and soak for twenty minutes to soothe muscle pain.
- Sleep. Your body needs time to heal. Ensure you get enough shut-eye.
- Go outside. Fresh air will clear your head and improve your mood.
- Stay hydrated to flush out toxins.
- Make laundry detergent from baking soda, bar soap, borax, and essential oils to save money.
- Switch to plant-based foods to reduce environmental impact and improve health.
- Recycle and compost whenever possible. This helps reduce waste and can help you save the environment.
- Use a rubber band to organize cables and avoid tangles.
- Store cords and chargers in a shoebox to keep them organized.
- Use a shower curtain to protect furniture from water damage or dust when you're away.
- For a thicker smoothie, freeze bananas before you blend them.
- Use a mason jar to store leftovers, keep them fresh, and prevent sogginess.

- Set a timer to turn off the lights when you're not home.
- Program your thermostat to save energy and reduce your carbon footprint.
- Reduce plastic waste by using a reusable water bottle.
- Invest in a canvas tote bag instead of a plastic bag to reduce plastic waste and look stylish.
- Bring a reusable shopping bag to the grocery store to go green and help you save.
- Commute by bike or public transportation to lower carbon impact and get exercise.
- Be kind and stay positive. Treat people kindly and have a sunny disposition. You will improve the world around you and feel good.

Follow these home remedy tips to make life easier and be environmentally friendly.

EASY HOME REMEDIES

Remember to consult your healthcare provider if your symptoms persist or if you have underlying health conditions.

✓ For nausea or motion sickness
Sniff or drink peppermint tea to help alleviate nausea and motion sickness.

✓ To soothe muscle pain
Mix a 1:1 ratio of olive oil and lavender essential oil, and massage the mixture onto sore muscles for a natural pain relief.

✓ To treat a common cold
Mix a 1:1 ratio of honey and fresh lemon juice. Take a spoonful as needed to soothe a cough and sore throat.

✓ For headache relief
Drink a glass of grape juice, or apply a warm compress to your forehead or on the back of your neck to alleviate a minor headache.

✓ Treat a sore throat
Mix ½ teaspoon of salt in 8 ounces of warm water, and gargle several times daily to soothe a sore throat.

✓ For upset stomachs
Drink ginger tea to help relieve nausea and indigestion.

✓ Get rid of bad breath
Create a solution with 1 teaspoon of baking soda in 8 ounces of water. Gargle and rinse to take care of odors and freshen your breath.

✓ Treat acne spots
Dilute a dab of tea tree oil with coconut oil (1:1 ratio), and apply a small amount onto acne spots to help kill bacteria and reduce inflammation.

7

Beauty Treatments

"Beauty is when you can appreciate yourself. When you love yourself, that's when you're most beautiful."

—Zoe Kravitz [9]

From an early age, many of us learned the importance of hygiene. Our health depends on it.

How we look and smell can positively or negatively impact our peers and coworkers. It leaves a lasting impression on who we are. Good hygiene keeps us from getting sick and influences our body image, self-esteem, and confidence.

Beauty is what is inside you. While you should shower every day and practice good grooming habits, how you look and what you do with your physical image is no one's business but your own. It's important to look clean and tidy regardless of your personal style. The following are simple suggestions to aid you in your daily routine.

93

Take Care of Your Appearance

You don't have to break the bank when you invest in your appearance. Adopt cost-friendly methods that bring out the best on a budget.

Establish a straightforward skin care routine with affordable products. Look for inexpensive skin care brands or try natural remedies at home. Drink plenty of water to keep your skin hydrated, and stick to a healthy diet. Buy marked-down shampoos, conditioners, and hair masks. Learn how to style hair to save money on trips to the salon.

Build a smart wardrobe and shop the clearance sales, visit thrift stores, or explore online marketplaces for secondhand clothes in excellent condition. Mix and match outfits and get creative to help each outfit go a long way, and accessorize without overspending.

Stay well-groomed and maintain good personal hygiene. Shower regularly, brush your teeth, and trim your nails. Invest in essential tools like a manicure kit and razor and keep a consistent schedule.

Watch your body language and posture when around others. Practice confidence when you stand, and maintain a good mien and ergonomic posture when you work. This will enhance your appearance, improve your health, and make you feel more self-assured.

In the interest of not looking like you're about to audition for a zombie movie, get enough sleep. Prioritize rest to avoid dark under-eye circles and puffiness. Establish a consistent sleep schedule and practice good sleep hygiene to contribute to overall health. Explore DIY beauty treatments such as homemade face masks, hair masks, and body scrubs. Many ingredients—such as honey, yogurt, oatmeal, and coconut oil—are likely already in your kitchen.

Your appearance isn't solely about how you look. It's about inner confidence and positivity. Cultivate self-respect, maintain a positive mindset, and practice self-care. Confidence and positivity significantly impact how you present to the world, and how you feel about yourself affects your mental health.

Remember that at the end of the day, happiness with your overall appearance means you feel good about yourself. While these tips will help you get the best look on a budget, make sure to embrace your unique

Daily Maintenance

Wash your face with an oil-free face wash every morning and night. Use an exfoliant scrub every other day to prevent acne and whiteheads from forming. Exfoliating will help keep your skin smooth and clean.

Moisturize

Aside from maintaining a healthy diet, drinking lots of water, and taking multivitamins, moisturizing your skin is also essential. Use a daily facial moisturizer to keep your skin young and healthy. There are various facial moisturizer products for both men and women. Find what product works best for your skin type and apply lotion or oil to your joints (knees, ankles, elbows, shoulders, and wrists).

Sunscreen

Use sunscreen every day, even on cloudy days. Proper sunscreen protects the skin from the sun's harmful rays and staves off premature aging, wrinkles, and skin cancer.

Makeup

Don't be afraid to experiment with different looks. Makeup is rule-free—have fun and find what works best for you. Wear makeup that matches your skin type. If you have an oily complexion, look for oil-free and non-comedogenic makeup that will not clog pores. If you have dry skin, look for hydrating and moisturizing makeup.

Waxing (For Women)

There are many alternatives to removing facial hair, such as tweezing, hair removal cream, and waxing. If you prefer to wax, wax your eyebrows and upper lip area once a month (or have a salon do it). Keep a pair of tweezers handy in your purse to pluck stray hairs from unwanted spots on your face.

Facials

Facials are a fantastic way to get pampered, rejuvenate your complexion, and promote a healthy glow. However, professional facials come with a ritzy bill, a luxury not everyone can afford. The good news is that several alternatives are available to help you save on facials. Let's explore ways to rejuvenate without depleting your wallet.

BEAUTY COLLEGE SALONS

Beauty college salons offer a fantastic opportunity to receive high-quality facials at a fraction of the average price. Cosmetology and aesthetician students, under the guidance of experienced instructors, staff these facilities. While the students are still trainees, they operate under close supervision and ensure you receive safe and satisfactory treatments. Beauty college salons often offer facial services, exfoliation, masks, and massages. Beauty colleges only let the students who are advanced enough in aesthetics perform the facials, and their grades depend on it. Beauty salons are the best way to get pampered and support the students if you want to treat yourself but are on a budget.

LOCAL SPA DEALS AND SPECIALS

Watch for local promotional deals, offers, and specials at nearby spas and wellness centers. Many establishments provide seasonal discounted rates or as a reward for loyalty programs. Sign up for newsletters, follow social media accounts, check their website for the latest deals, and get discounted facials.

Group Booking Discounts

Invite family or friends to join you for a facial. Many spas and salons give group booking discounts. Enjoy a day at the spa with loved ones while you save money. Some resorts may offer private packages where you receive treatments and enjoy exclusive use of the spa at discounted rates.

Home Facials

Never fear if you can't afford a spa treatment and options are limited. Create a revitalizing spa day from home. Home facials are a great alternative to commercial facials. Take the time to investigate the type of skin care products you want and research skin care recipes and the best techniques for your skin type. DIY facials involve more effort than being treated at a luxurious spa, but still, a spa day at home allows you to customize the experience any way you want without any extra charges or hassle. So turn on some spa music, light a few candles, place those cucumber slices over your eyes, and enjoy a home facial.

Free Community Facials

This option involves keeping both eyes open for opportunities, but it's worth it. Stay current on community events or charity programs that offer discounted or free facials. Local organizations, beauty schools, or aesthetician training programs sponsor these events to give back to the community. Such events provide an opportunity to experience a free facial and contribute to a good cause.

Proper skin care in your youth helps prevent skin problems in the future and keeps skin looking young and fit. You can have healthy skin if you explore options and make intelligent choices.

Grape-Seed Oil for Beauty Treatments

Grape-seed oil is a wonderful tool. You can use it on your whole body after a shower; it works better than lotion to keep your skin smooth and tight. Health stores have 100 percent grape-seed oil for skin, which is the best route, but store-bought oil in the baking section also works.

Hair

Use extra virgin coconut oil as hair oil. If you want long hair, coconut oil helps hair to grow. Place a jar in a bowl of hot water. Pour the desired amount on dry hair, wear a shower cap (or plastic grocery bag) for an hour or longer, clean with shampoo and conditioner, and rinse. Doing this once a week or even twice a month promotes a healthy shine and will help your hair grow faster.

Do a deep condition at least once a week. Put conditioner on your hair, cover it with a shower cap while in the shower (while you shave or do something else), let it steam for about ten minutes, then rinse. Tea tree oil conditioners are best for this and help with itchy scalps. If you have tea tree oil, add a bit to your shampoo to help itchy scalps.

Sunshine, water, and vitamins (or eating healthy food) help your hair reach its fullest potential, just like photosynthesis for plants. If you want long, shiny hair with a lot of volume and gloss, try to shower when your hair can dry naturally. Using a blow-dryer damages your hair. You can blow-dry your hair and use a curling iron once a week, but avoid overuse.

After showering, use a paddle brush to detangle and straighten your hair, then let it dry naturally for an hour or two. Brush again and style. A key to knowing the health of your hair is to gauge how quickly it dries after being wet. The longer it takes to dry, the better. A sign of damaged hair or split ends is hair that dries instantly. Have the ends of your hair trimmed a quarter of an inch once every month to promote growth and health.

Look for shampoos and conditioners made from natural, organic, or vegetable ingredients, and use a small amount when you wash. Use grapefruit or lemon oil for greasy hair, sandalwood or rose for dry hair, and tea tree for dandruff.

Manicure with Paraffin Wax Bath

1. Wash and sanitize your hands.
2. Remove any polish.
3. File and shape your nails.

CHAPTER 7: BEAUTY TREATMENTS

4. Soak your hands in a manicure bowl. (This can be tea tree oil or grape-seed oil.)
5. Apply an exfoliating cuticle treatment.
6. Press back the eponychium (the half-moon-shaped portion of the nail nearest the skin) and remove cuticle tissue or any lingering substance.
7. Neutralize with NAS 99%.
8. Buff your nails.
9. Apply cuticle oil.
10. Massage with finishing butter for 5–8 minutes.
11. Dip your hands in paraffin wax, cover with a plastic bag and mittens, and let it set for at least 5 minutes.
12. Remove the wax from your hands once cooled down.
13. Clean the nail plate with NAS 99%.
14. Balance pH with Bond Aid.
15. Apply a clear base coat.
16. Apply two layers of lacquer.
17. Apply a top coat and any decals or nail art as you wish.
18. Let it dry, and enjoy!

Foot Soak Home Remedy

If you participate in vigorous physical activity, chances are you'll get sore feet and possibly fungus-related foot conditions. At the dollar store, purchase one plastic bedpan or rectangular dishwashing tub large enough to accommodate your feet, a bottle of white vinegar, and a peppermint mouthwash bottle.

Add a 1:1 ratio of vinegar and mouthwash (I recommend 1/3 of each bottle). Fill the tub or bedpan halfway with warm water and the vinegar-mouthwash solution, with enough foot soak to cover your feet. It should foam up. Soak your feet for fifteen minutes or until all bubbles subside, then dry your feet and enjoy the tingling effect. Vinegar gets rid of the fungus, and this is an enjoyable soak for tired feet after exercising. It also prevents athletes' foot and fungi from developing. Keep your feet clean and toenails filed down and clipped. Change your socks twice a day.

Vanilla Brown Sugar Body Scrub

Create a homemade body scrub from the ingredients below and store it in a small jar or container. These also make great party gifts.

- 2 cups brown sugar
- 1 cup granulated sugar
- 1 cup sunflower oil
- 1 Tbsp. vanilla extract

Alternative Sugar Scrub

Makes: 1½ cups

Ingredients:

- 1 cup sugar or other granulated sweeteners
- 1 cup oil of choice (organic grape-seed or avocado oil)
- 2–4 drops of essential oils (I recommend lavender)

Method:

1. Combine all ingredients in a bowl.
2. Stir to combine.
3. Store in a small jar or glass container. Essential oils can damage plastic, and metals change the properties of the oils.

Chafing

Yeah, it's gross, but if you wear any uniform or scrubs and tend to work long hours, you'll experience chafing at some point. There are two remedies for this:

1. Try sprinkling a small amount of unscented baby powder on the affected area and a tiny bit on your underwear. Keep a miniature travel-size bottle in your purse or work bag to use when needed (and seal it in a sandwich bag).

CHAPTER 7: BEAUTY TREATMENTS

2. If the chafing is near your upper thigh and is worse than usual after a long shift, try treating it with a generic jock itch cream to reduce the swelling.

If the symptoms persist, see a doctor.

True Beauty

The biggest takeaway about beauty is to be confident in your own skin. True beauty doesn't discriminate based on looks, shape, or size. Whatever your situation, embrace your inner beauty, feel secure, and love yourself for who you are.

SKINCARE
Checklist

TIME: | DAY:

DAY TIME

NIGHT TIME

- ☐
- ☐
- ☐
- ☐
- ☐
- ☐
- ☐
- ☐

REMINDER

SHOPPING LIST

- ☐ Daily Face Wash
- ☐ Exfoliant
- ☐ Moisturizer - Day and Night
- ☐ Toner
- ☐ Under Eye Cream

8

"I never travel without my diary. One should always have something sensational to read in the train."

—Oscar Wilde [10]

One of the most incredible milestones in feeling like an independent adult is traveling. Traveling improves your well-being, decreases the risk of heart attack and anxiety, and stimulates your brain.

Can you remember a specific taste or smell from your travels? I remember savoring the delightful flavors of a tomato and basil strudel from a vendor at the Hauptbahnhof, a spot I frequented before catching trains in Germany; a buttery, flaky baguette I ate in Paris; and a delicious lamb roast dinner in an ancient English pub in Canterbury. I also remember opening an MRE ("Meal, Ready-to-Eat") for the first time in the Army—who could forget that? What an experience!

Travel has a positive impact on our hearts and mental health. Exploring a new place increases dopamine in your brain, stimulating your neurotransmission and brain activity.

Traveling is a fantastic way to meet new people, gain fresh perspectives, and uplift yourself personally. You might travel because of business, go with a few of your friends to Disneyland or Europe, or explore somewhere you've never been. Here are a few tips for when you do decide to travel.

Travel in a Group or with a Friend

Never travel alone. Both single men and women are abducted and targeted. Even with technology at our fingertips with cell phones and Wi-Fi, don't risk something happening to you. Always travel with one or more people.

Tell Someone Where You're Going

Headed out of town for a weekend away? Are you going to the mountains, a cabin, or the lake to get off the grid? Let someone close to you know. If you get injured or there's an accident and no one knows where you are, they won't know they need to look for you or *where* to look for you. Traveling alone could have severe consequences. If you go to the store, leave a Post-it Note on the fridge or send a text.

Don't Place Yourself in Dangerous Areas or Situations

Travel with friends, and if you go to a club, go to one with a good security team in a decent, clean area. Don't put yourself in harm's way or scary situations. If something feels wrong, trust your gut, leave, and go somewhere safe. Think of yourself as your private security liaison and choose safe avenues.

Preparation is the Name of the Game

Before you travel, do your homework and learn as much as possible about the destination. Preparation and research will help you make the most of the trip and avoid surprises. Not everything will go as planned when you travel, so go prepared. Pack for all kinds of weather and have a backup plan in case of flight cancellations. Keep calm when you run into snags, and know the local customs and laws.

Here are some things to consider when you're preparing for a trip:

- Do research.

- Consult your budget.
- Pack smart.
- Consider your clothes.
- Check your travel guide and local websites for your destination.

Stay Open-Minded ("When in Rome . . .")

Travel is an excellent opportunity to learn about cultures and meet people. Be open to fresh experiences and step outside your comfort zone. When you travel, be safe. Stay mindful of your surroundings and take precautions. Remain aware of personal items, stay in well-lit areas, and do not walk alone at night.

Above all, have a good time. Travel is supposed to be enjoyable, so relax and let loose. Take time to explore, step outside the box, and make memories to last a lifetime.

Here are some additional tips:

- Try not to travel in peak season. Peak season means higher prices and larger crowds.
- Consider hostels or guesthouses. Research beforehand to make sure the establishment has good reviews and is in a safe area. Hostels and guesthouses can save you money on accommodations and are a terrific way to meet people.
- Travel with someone you know to make the experience more enjoyable and safer.
- Cook meals, especially if you're on a budget. Cooking meals cuts costs and offers a unique look into the local grocers and food cultures wherever you visit.
- Take advantage of free activities. Many cities have free foot tours, museums, and other activities.
- Try to learn basic phrases in the local language to complete simple transactions. This can go a long way.
- Dress appropriately and be respectful of the local culture. Avoid taking photos of people without consent and stay mindful of local customs.
- Leave no trace. When you travel, pack out trash and respect the environment.

Commuting

As a young adult in today's fast-paced world, you're always on the move and need transportation. If you don't have a car or it's more convenient to commute, there's excellent news—you have options. From an array of rentable e-scooters and bikes to buses, local trains, and ride-share programs, getting around these days is easier than ever.

Let's explore the available options.

BIKES

Biking is a healthy, viable, and efficient mode of transportation if you'd like to get fresh air and exercise on the way to work. Some buses also offer bike racks to help cyclists commute more efficiently for longer distances.

Pros	Cons
Cost-effective and affordable Extensive coverage and suitable for both long and short commutes Eco-friendly and greener environmental impact since they reduce the number of cars on the road	Requires physical fitness and exertion, which may be challenging in rugged terrains Not weather friendly—inclement weather makes a commute difficult and more complicated when using a bike Limited storage—bikes have limited storage capacity, which is a drawback if you have to transport oversized items

BUSES

Buses are the historic go-to of public transport, with extensive route coverage that offers pickups in urban and suburban areas.

CHAPTER 8: TRAVELING

Pros	Cons
Cost-effective and affordable Extensive coverage and suitable for both long and short commutes Eco-friendly and greener environmental impact since they reduce the number of cars on the road	Fixed schedules—riders must consult the predetermined routes and be on time (and bear in mind buses may miss a stop on occasion) Congestion and traffic, which could lead to delays Crowds, limited seats, and possible discomfort if passengers must stand

RENTABLE E-SCOOTERS

If you've gone outside recently, chances are you've seen a person buzz around on an e-scooter. Popular in cities and suburbs, convenient and eco-friendly, e-scooters are a click away on any smartphone app, available for rent by the minute.

Pros	Cons
Affordable Cost-flexible with pay-as-you-go models Easy to use with minimal effort Efficient for short distances and quick trips City-friendly	Limited range and battery life Limited availability because they are high in demand Safety concerns—riders must use caution

TRAINS

Local trains are another staple in the transportation infrastructure in many cities, offering both comfort and convenience to many passengers.

Pros	Cons
Ideal for longer commutes and efficient for travel between cities or neighborhoods Reliable travel times—trains arrive at destinations quicker because they are on their own rail Comfortable and spacious	Expense—trains tend to cost more than other public transport Crowded conditions—there may be standing room only when rush hour hits, which makes some passengers uncomfortable Noisiness from both the train tracks and fellow passengers may be an inconvenience

Disneyland

Disneyland is a popular and expensive destination, but it's possible to make a trip affordable through careful planning and smart choices. Here are some tips to help you save at Disneyland:

- **Plan ahead.** Book the park tickets, hotel, and transport in advance to take advantage of early bird discounts, promos, and special offers. Don't be afraid to pick a hotel further away from Disneyland. Check if the hotel has a shuttle service (like ART—Anaheim Resort Transportation) before you book. The ART stops near the ticket booth areas at the parks.
- **Visit during off-peak seasons.** Avoid peak times and visit during non-holiday weekdays and off-peak seasons for a less crowded experience and to save money on tickets and accommodations. Pick a hotel that offers a complimentary breakfast, free parking, a fridge, and a microwave. When you first arrive at the hotel room, wipe down surfaces the hotel crew might have missed: light switches, TV remote control, telephone, doorknobs,

CHAPTER 8: TRAVELING

bedside alarm clock, and the toilet flush handle. Despite the hotel's amenities, germs still exist and housekeeping isn't always thorough.

- **See about discounted tickets.** Look for discounted park tickets through authorized ticket resellers, travel agencies, or group deals. Never buy from unauthorized sellers, as they could be counterfeit. Don't pick the park hopper option. One park per day will save you money when you purchase for several days, and there is more than enough to do in one park per day, allowing you to have more fun.
- **Bring your food and drinks.** Disneyland allows visitors to bring food and nonalcoholic drinks into the park, so pack a lunch and snacks for later. Make a list of food and beverages before driving to the hotel (e.g., bottled water, instant tuna, cracker kits, noodles, bread, PB&J ingredients, chips, fruit snacks, juice boxes). On the day you go into the park, pack enough for everyone to have lunch and snacks, then splurge on a nice dinner in the park or maybe fun park treats. Take a backpack into the park and pack sandwiches, chips, and drinks. Freeze a water bottle overnight. It will stay cold, work overtime as an ice pack, and keep the rest of the food fresh. Restaurants in Disneyland will also fill your water bottle for free.
- **Take a break and eat outside the park.** Usually, by mid- to late-afternoon, park visitors want to take a break. If you're limited by how much you have to spend, consider eating a complimentary breakfast for free at the hotel before you enter the park, having a packed lunch in the middle of the day, and exploring nearby affordable restaurants for dinner.
- **Buy refillable drinking cups.** The parks offer refillable drinking cups that can save money to get refills throughout the day.
- **Souvenirs and toys.** Avoid unnecessary souvenirs or your budget will buckle beneath the weight of the purchases. Limit how much you plan to spend and stick to it. Hit the dollar store for toys and souvenirs before the trip. They sell many Disney products. This method will give you more money to buy one nice toy or gift in the park per person while still having fun souvenirs. You can save a ton from the dollar store when you get princess wands or glow sticks, autograph books, Disney knockoff trinkets, and so on.

- **The essentials.** Protection is necessary if you plan to get wet on the water rides or stand in the sun, which is pretty much anywhere in Disneyland. Bring essentials from home rather than overpay for sunscreen, ponchos, handheld fans, and other items.
- **Utilize Disney websites and apps.** Visit Disneyland's official apps and website to learn the ins, the outs, and the options. Look into the rates for wait times, entertainment schedules, and dining options. Use these resources to plan your day efficiently and you will minimize unnecessary waiting and maximize fun.
- **Plan for extra costs.** If you're interested in a fun add-on experience, like a princess meet and greet or character dining, be mindful of extra fees. Disneyland offers various additional experiences and services. Prioritize spending, and budget beforehand.

You can still have a memorable, fun experience when you plan and make wise financial choices. Be financially slender, not a spender.

PACKING CHECKLIST

TRIP DATES _____

CLOTHING & ACCESSORIES	✔
Bras	
Casual Shirts	
Dress Shirts	
Hiking Boots	
Jeans	
Leisure Boots	
Pants	
Sleepwear	
Sneakers/Shoes	
Socks	
T-Shirts	
Underwear	

TOILETRIES	✔
Dental Floss	
Deodorant	
Facial Cleanser	
Hairbrush and Comb	
Moisturizer	
Sanitary Napkins/Tampons	
Shampoo and Conditoner	
Soap or Body Wash	
Styling Tools	
Sunscreen	
Toothbrush	
Toothpaste	

MISCELLANEOUS	✔
Banking Contact/Information	
Cell Phone	
Laptop/Tablet	
List of Medications	
Portable Power Bank/Charger	

CARRY-ON ITEMS	✔
Earbuds/Headphones	
Eye Mask and Earplugs	
Passport	
Tissues	
Travel Pillow	

9

Life Advice

*"No matter what people tell you, words
and ideas can change the world."*

—Robin Williams [11]

THE EXCITING PART ABOUT YOUR LIFE ADVENTURE IS THAT YOU'RE JUST starting. You can come from nothing and from it fashion everything. If you take away one thing from this book, I hope it's this: From this point on, your past doesn't matter. What you do from this moment on does.

Get Up and Get Moving

Begin each day with a sense of purpose. Have a plan about the tasks you most want to tackle before you go to sleep, and endeavor to wake up with the motivation to complete them, preferably before noon. Act as if you have something fresh to learn each day, and inevitably you will.

In *Daily Rituals: How Artists Work* by Mason Currey,[12] the author shares his research on the habits of famous writers, artists, and musicians. Each one of their daily routines held something interesting in common—they were all the most productive, creative, and motivated first thing in the morning, getting most of their tasks and pursuits accomplished before noon.

"Early to bed, early to rise" are words to live by. Getting enough rest to rejuvenate your body and feel healthy and ready to go in the morning is vital to your emotional and physical health.

Always start your day on a good note, with an attitude of gratitude. Keep an open mind and a sunny disposition. Eat healthy, and exercise if possible. Create a motivational playlist of songs that uplift or inspire you that you can listen to either as you work out or in your daily commute. Tune in to relevant talk shows or podcasts that encourage you. By putting a soundtrack to your life as you go about your day, you'll feel good and have something to look forward to each day when you get up.

Read Your Head Off

Take at least fifteen minutes each day to read. Read a brochure, an essay, a helpful article or magazine, or a book. Whatever you are into, reading each day isn't just for elementary kids. Reading improves our perception of life and mental health.

When you read an insightful article or book, endeavor to read it slowly and retain the knowledge, wisdom, and advice it gives you. Highlight parts you consider important and relevant to your life and any useful excerpts that could benefit you.

Reading will lure you out of your comfort zone, teach you new things, and give you ideas for the future. No matter where you are, who you are, or how old you are, never stop learning.

Learn from the Wisdom of Others

We live in a culture where memes of "Okay, Boomer" may score a laugh. However, people who lived through the Great Depression, the Vietnam War, and the Cold War Era have undergone a radical technological transformation that will blow your mind if you think about it long enough. The older generation has hard-core work ethics and resilient attitudes, and they understand true adversity. Listen to the advice and wisdom of generations before you.

CHAPTER 9: LIFE ADVICE

The older generation possesses a treasure trove of excellent advice about frugal living and maintaining a positive attitude during hard times. Back then, it was a way of life and a necessity.

If you have an elderly loved one or teacher in your life, take every opportunity to learn from them as much as possible. Read books on highly effective habits in the workplace and the healthy practices of octogenarians. The book *Ikigai: The Japanese Secret to a Long and Happy Life*[13] delves into expert advice from Japanese people who have lived to be over a hundred years old.

A common emerging theme in the advice you'll find from those who have lived a long and happy life is being grateful, being up and moving, and being social. When you can glean wisdom and learn what the past teaches you, you will be wiser and better prepared to balance your life choices.

Your Sense of Wonder Is Your Shield

While it's important to assert yourself and stick to your guns when it comes to doing the right thing, try to stay open to change and malleable as you learn and grow. Retain your sense of wonder and find small pleasures rather than negativity or stubbornness. As you keep your mind and heart open, you'll feel good inside and discover little joys along your growing journey. Life is what you make it, and your attitude and outlook play a big part in the ultimate shape of who you become. Find fun in your tasks and activities. As you mature into adulthood, remember what it was like to be a child and stay playful. Keep your spark.

Build Your Support System

The overall effect of a support system on a person's mental health can make a tremendous positive impact, paving the way for happiness and success.

Everyone needs someone to believe in them, even if it's just one person. You deserve a meaningful connection with someone who cheers you on and uplifts you in good times and bad. Each person's support system will look different because we all come from different walks of life. While someone might have eighteen friends and a hugely supportive family, another person may have one dear, close friend to whom they confide. Neither one is better than the other. We all have different paths to walk in life, and comparing your life to someone else's will never make you happy. Understand that your journey is uniquely yours.

When feasible, reach out to family and friends. We have a wealth of technology at our fingertips, where people are only a text, social media comment, or phone call away.

If you already have a support system of nurturing friends, hold on to them and be thankful. If you have a hard time building your support system, try other methods that can help: enroll in a support group that pertains to you or investigate hiking groups, reading clubs, gyms, Zumba classes, or community gardening.

You'll find someone you connect with who understands and appreciates you for you.

Set Goals

Be self-motivated and continually set achievable goals. If you can dream it, you can do it. Goals and success are the ultimate mental power couple. Reaching our goals helps give us a sense of purpose and self-esteem, and fulfilling the goals we set for ourselves improves our quality of life.

Volunteer!

Volunteering is a powerful lesson in selfless service. Everyone has varying levels of experience as a natural volunteer. Some were born with an inherent selfless disposition. Some learn through trial and error or a humbling experience. Some don't get the opportunity to understand what it means to be selfless until they have children. Whichever category you fit into, try to the best of your ability to help others as much as possible.

Volunteering in the community is a great way to learn valuable lessons in selflessness. Developing selflessness early on will jump-start you for success and happiness. Volunteering helps not only those around you and people in need, but it also reduces stress, keeps you mentally stimulated, and reduces depression. We increase our compassion and awareness for our fellow man as we serve others, bringing immeasurable joy to both them and ourselves.

Does your local homeless shelter need someone to chop vegetables for an afternoon? Does the animal shelter need someone to come in and cuddle the cats and dogs? Does your teacher need help passing out papers? Get in there and lend a hand. Volunteering is usually something you can list on your resume. It doesn't take a massive amount of time. You'll have greater happiness when you give your time to others and learn how rewarding it can be.

Suppose you have children and volunteer as a room parent at their school for an hour. Teachers need the support of moms and dads in the classroom, and your child won't forget the day mom or dad came in to help. Volunteering is fun, and it builds lasting memories.

Your Home, Your Palace

Your home should be your special place. Home should be a place of safety and security, where you can feel comfortable and steady no matter what is happening in the world. Even if you live in the tiniest New York apartment that ever existed, live well. Create a calm, serene, stabilizing environment that cheers you up and calms you down.

On Interviewing

Before going to a job interview, look online and research the company's history, mission, and goals. The biggest goal in an interview is to present your best professional self. Be sure to silence your cell phone during any interview.

Dress for success and be punctual. Make eye contact, smile, and shake hands with your interviewer(s), but don't act overly familiar or loosey-goosey.

Use the proper etiquette for the situation and be open and honest in all your responses. Take notes and show that you're actively listening and engaged with your body language. Avoid fidgeting or nervous ticks. If you don't know the answer to an interview question, say so, but show your willingness to learn or find out.

When they ask you to tell them about yourself, don't shy away from listing your strengths. Now is the time to sell yourself and show why you'd be a perfect fit. Maintain a positive, upbeat demeanor throughout the interview, and thank them for their time.

Remember that job hunting has hits and misses, and you will eventually find the right home for your talents.

Start Your Workday with Rituals

Daily rituals can help level us out. They serve as a buffer against uncertainty and anxiety and help put your energy in proper order. Do you get to work and check your email or calendar first thing? Do you write down the tasks you want to accomplish? Getting into positive routines can streamline you for success and effective decision-making while helping increase your focus on essential duties.

On Good Work Ethic

Having a good work ethic means something at the end of the day. Companies hire employees based on their skill set and the type of person they present themselves to be. Be punctual and on time for your job. Don't do anything you shouldn't do or take longer lunch breaks than needed. Start each day with a fresh pair of eyes and a positive attitude. Don't take your position for granted.

Being honest and hardworking pays off, period. You must do what's right legally and morally and treat others respectfully. Also, remember that change is good, and moving to another position or company can bring opportunities you might not have anywhere else.

Calling in to Work Sick

If you're sick, you're sick. Call in when you're honestly ill, and don't risk spreading a nasty cold, fever, flu, or COVID-19 to someone else. It's the courteous thing to do. Taking care of yourself is a first-and-foremost priority. That said, avoid calling in to work sick if you have something minor like a tickly throat or mild cough or just don't feel like working. Laziness can develop into bad habits and jeopardize your job.

Check Your Benefits

Get into the habit of checking your benefit information, glancing at your pay stub online, and perusing your 401k portfolio from time to time. Ensure that all your information is up to date and that the paychecks accurately reflect hours worked, holiday pay, overtime, and so on. Open enrollment falls under an annual deadline with each company for health benefits. Stay aware of these dates and comply with enrolling so you don't miss out on your benefits and insurance.

Employee Discounts

Take advantage of employee discounts. Enjoy a restaurant meal or any percentage off oil change services for being an employee of your company—flash that work badge and save money. If your work has a list of companies that will give you a discount, use those opportunities and make the most of your perks and discounts.

Tuition Reimbursement

While filling out paperwork and chasing down people for signatures can be a pain, it's worth getting reimbursed for tuition costs. If your work offers reimbursement for college, no matter how little, *go after it*. It's worth waiting out slow turnaround times for every extra cent toward your education. If you already have a grant or scholarship for school, that is even more reason to get reimbursed, as the money could help pay groceries and bills.

Work Etiquette

Act mature and polite at work. You're not there to flirt or date, so avoid romantic entanglements with coworkers, especially managers. If you jell with someone and things work out outside office hours, that's great, but be professional and respectful when you're on the clock. Your peers and colleagues will respond if you have an approachable, open persona.

Treat others the way you'd like them to treat you. Keep political and religious discussions outside work, as it can make people uncomfortable and build animosity. Be sensitive to the needs of others, and assess each situation tactfully. Are your actions appropriate for the workplace? Are you a team player and make everyone feel included? Set a good example in your role.

Ask questions and participate in meetings. You'll only grow and progress if you stay inquisitive and seek to learn more. If you're not sure about something, ask. While no one wants to babysit their colleague, it's okay to ask for help or another opinion to understand something better. Regarding work-related issues, don't let timidity inhibit your need to know so that you can do your job effectively.

Don't gossip. The old saying "If you can't say something nice, don't say anything at all" rings true. Gossiping gets people into trouble and creates rifts. Don't cause drama or get involved in it. Be pleasant and courteous to others and focus on your job. Kindness goes a long way.

Time Management

Be careful how you manage your time while working. Our busy world has so many distractions that getting overwhelmed and off track with your work assignments is easy. Endeavor to have as few tabs open on your computer as possible. Don't open another tab unless you've completed your specific task. Keep your work area free of clutter and clear any messes before you end your day.

CHAPTER 9: LIFE ADVICE

If you get distracted too quickly, consider what is distracting you. Schedule a time (either on break or during out-of-office hours) to set aside for social media, texting, or whichever diversion is holding you back from being more productive.

Side Hustles

Many people have second jobs to make their rent or mortgage payments. If you're lucky enough to have something non-work-related that you're passionate about that brings in a little extra income, explore that! Start a hobby outside of work that you enjoy, even if it doesn't make you any money at first.

A side hustle can help you decide what you want to do with your life.

Perhaps you spotlight as a street artist on the weekends, sing gigs with a band on Saturdays, cook gluten-free baked treats, or do freelance designs or graphics. Don't be afraid to dabble and explore these skills and talents. Side projects can bring in extra needed income while offering you a glimpse into your future. Most adults go through five or six career changes in their lives.

On Entitlement

Being attractive or desirable to the eye isn't a character trait—it comes down to genetics and has to do with dominant and recessive genes shaping your physical characteristics. If someone is prettier, more handsome, or more prosperous than you, it doesn't make them better. Some are luckier than others when it comes to the genetic lottery. In the long run, what matters is how you treat people, how kind you are, and the goodness in your heart. In the words of Judge Judy, "Beauty fades, but dumb is forever."[14]

Focus first on shaping your soul and outlook on life in a positive light, and no matter what you look like, your inner beauty will shine outward for all the world to see.

Remember this quote by Roald Dahl: "If a person has ugly thoughts, it begins to show on the face. And when that person has ugly thoughts every day, every week, every year, the face gets uglier and uglier until you can hardly bear to look at it. A person who has good thoughts cannot ever be ugly. You can have a wonky nose and a crooked mouth and a double chin and stick-out teeth, but if you have good thoughts, it will shine out of your face like sunbeams and you will always look lovely."[15]

You WILL Experience Hardship

There will be times when unfair, horrible things happen, even when your intentions are good and your heart is true—even when you're trying your best and you don't deserve it. Bad things happen to good people. People we love are taken from us too soon. Pets, loved ones, and even children die. Pain is what makes us, and adversity shapes us. What you must decide is how you're going to deal with it.

In 2007, Christopher Williams drove home on the freeway from an evening basketball game. A drunk seventeen-year-old smashed into his minivan, killing his son, daughter, and pregnant wife. Only he and his small son survived. Rather than choose to live his life in grief and anger, Mr. Williams forgave the boy and wrote a book called *Let It Go*.[16] He eventually remarried and found peace and love despite his tragedy.

Hardship is a part of life, and it will happen to everyone.

When you face adversity, you have two choices: you can give up, or you can deal with the pain then try harder. You can't always control what happens to you, but the one thing you *do* have control of and a say in is how you deal with it. Seek professional help in dealing with any grief or loss. Find what brings you peace and comfort in life.

You Have the Power to Stop the Cycle of Abuse

Suppose you were in an abusive relationship with your parents, caregivers, or significant others, or you currently find yourself in a toxic relationship. In that case, you have the power to heal your troubled heart and stop hurting. Remove yourself from any harmful situation and seek professional help at the nearest clinic, women's shelter, or through a professional therapist.

Talk about your emotions with someone safe who you trust, and tell them how you feel. Healing and happiness begin with you taking the first step. Do not keep yourself in a hostile environment. You deserve to be happy.

Don't Let Anyone Make You Cruel

If you have suffered physical, emotional, or sexual abuse, remember that you are entitled to happiness, which is within your grasp. You are in control of your life from here on out. Choose love. Be warm and have compassion for others. Choose dear friends and kindness. Treat yourself like you deserve, with tenderness and compassion. Once you've left your hostile environment or relationship, don't let the past scars create a roadblock to the future. Use your past hardship as a stepping stone to move forward and overcome it.

Life Is Not a Fairy Tale (Unless You Make It One)

In line with the message fairy tales gave us as children, "happily ever after" really does exist. Still, it's more of a state of mind and self-love than a handsome prince or beautiful princess rescuing us and whisking us away to their expensive castle in the clouds. The journey won't be all green lights, but it will be rewarding. For many successful, happy people, a fairy tale comes from enduring a little longer, working a lot harder, and keeping a positive self-image with their results in mind.

Always assume full responsibility for your happiness. You can achieve whatever you're willing to work hard enough to achieve, but it's up to you to make it happen. In everything you do, you're limited only by the power of your imagination. If you can find what makes you come alive and hold on to it, you *will* live happily ever after.

Don't Overthink Everything

Don't spend too much time analyzing or rehashing things in your head. Overthinking can rob you of the present and create undue stress and anxiety you don't need. If you find yourself mentally besieged by something stressing you out, go for a walk to help clear your mind.

It's Okay to Fail

The average young adult goes through five or six career changes before age thirty. It's okay if something you've dreamt about falls through. Perhaps you were meant to walk a different path. It doesn't mean you're any less unique or special. It means you're growing and about to embark on a different journey than you fantasized about as a teen. And that's okay. It's a normal part of life experience.

Failure is a good teacher and a powerful motivator. James Cameron started as a truck driver, and Harrison Ford was a blue-collar carpenter. J. K. Rowling was a teacher and single mom on welfare. Adam Driver got turned down when he first auditioned for the Juilliard School; he joined the Marines, and two years later, when he reauditioned for Juilliard, he got in.

Learn from Your Mistakes

Inevitably, everyone messes up. Despite how together or entitled people might act, nobody knows what they're doing when they first launch into adulthood. Everyone starts as a fish swimming in the same ocean against the same current. As the Alanis Morissette song goes, "No one's really got it figured out just yet."[17] Making mistakes is essential to learning and growing, and it's how we evolve.

Chapter 9: Life Advice

Make Amends

The Hippocratic oath doctors take upon getting their MD says, *"Primum non nocere,"* or "first, do no harm."[18] Whether you work in health care or not, adopt this ethos. Don't bring harm upon anyone or anything for any reason. Make it a part of your life.

Keeping that in mind, everyone makes mistakes.

We all do or say something we regret on occasion. If you do, try to do everything you can to make amends, whatever that means for your situation. Apologize if needed, reflect on what you could have done differently, dust off your pants, stand up, and keep moving forward. It is important not to dwell on the past—that's not your final destination. What matters is starting fresh and moving forward. Learn from your mistakes, become more aware and compassionate, and strive to make better choices in the future.

Social Media and Online Etiquette

Practice appropriate conduct online and be cautious. If you wouldn't say or do it in person, don't say or do it online. Social media can be fun and helpful, but do not share intensely personal details or oversensitive hardships. When paying a bill or doing a monetary transaction online, check that the window has an https:// prefix in the internet address—the added *s* means it's secure. Invest in antivirus software and malware to prevent your computer from getting a virus.

Speak Up

While it's essential to be sensitive to situations and filter your actions with others, don't be afraid to speak your mind. If you see something happening that's wrong or illegal, say something. If you see a crime committed or overt discrimination happening at work, report it to HR. If someone at work is harassing you, tell them it's inappropriate and speak to a manager. No one has the right to belittle you or mistreat you.

Actions Speak Louder Than Words

Your actions matter—every day, what you do *matters*. How you act and treat people leaves an impressionable footprint that shows others the content of your character and the strength of your heart. Be kind, treat others well, and aim to live a good life doing the right thing.

Happiness Is a Choice

Your happiness is dependent on *you*. You can land a great job, make money, and have a solid relationship with someone you love, but happiness is an inside job. If you can't be happy on your own and find pleasure in simple things, you can't be satisfied with other people. In the words of Abraham Lincoln, "Most people are about as happy as they make up their minds to be."[19] Love yourself, and others will love you.

Pursue Your Dreams

If you have a dream, pursue it. But stay realistic about what it takes to achieve it. You still need a roof over your head, have bills to pay, and need to eat. Dream your dreams to the fullest, keep your feet planted, and stay levelheaded. Walk *your* path, and never stop believing in yourself.

Fourteen Things to Remember

1. There will always be someone smarter, prettier, wealthier, luckier, skinnier, and more successful than you. Life isn't fair. Get over it and live the best life you can.
2. You cannot change the past. Learn from it and move forward.
3. Opinions don't define your reality.
4. Everyone's journey is different.
5. Things get better with time. Everything has a shelf life.
6. Judgments are a confession of character.
7. Overthinking will lead to sadness.

CHAPTER 9: LIFE ADVICE

8. Your happiness comes from within. Be happy with what you have.
9. Positive thoughts create positive things.
10. Smiles are contagious, and gratitude is a great multiplier.
11. Kindness and knowledge are free.
12. You only fail if you quit.
13. What goes around comes around.
14. No matter how bad you think you might have it, remember—you're living someone else's fairy tale. Count your blessings.

When Life Gets Tough

Choosing to walk away or try harder is one of the most complex decisions you'll ever face in a career or relationship. Deep down, you'll know whether whatever is in question is worth it. Whatever the struggle you face, if you believe in the result, stick through it, and try your best, it will turn out alright. Learn to question things and gain good common sense. Being grounded will help you navigate whatever challenges you face.

Remember that half of life's battle is endurance. Those who endure and hold on a little longer than others are the ones who wind up the happiest and most successful. Pray or meditate, and you'll find the answers you seek.

Dealing with Adversity

Being an adult means being proactive with your life, especially during adversity. If you want something, you have to work hard enough to achieve it. Adopting a positive, motivated mindset will help you move forward and succeed, especially when faced with setbacks.

Those who have tasted adversity earlier in life tend to function better as adults because they understand the concept of driving on.

If you're experiencing adversity for the first time or going through a situation you don't know how to handle, remember—*trials make you stronger*. They're necessary to hardwire us into being able to deal with stress. They help shape us and give us the tools to develop coping mechanisms as mature adults.

Developing your internal locus of control (how you deal with stressful scenarios) is pivotal. People with an internal locus of control believe they are responsible for their success and that they shape their future. Can you keep calm when everything around you falls apart or implodes? Can you stay centered and be helpful when someone has an emotional breakdown?

Find Your Inner Peace

For some people, inner peace is yoga, meditation, or prayer. For others, it's writing, painting, or composing a song. For some, it's taking a walk or spending five minutes alone in the bathroom to breathe. Whatever that means for you, discover what calms you and helps you stay focused. But it's crucial to stay clear and focused when problems arise, have a positive attitude, and project your attitude onto others. Adversity dies down— lasting impressions from how you handle it never do.

Stop Complaining

When we were small children and scraped our knees on the pavement, we limped toward our caregivers for comfort and first aid. We wailed loudly, "I have a boo-boo!" We were immediately attended to, coddled, and sent on our merry way back out to play. Adulthood isn't quite the same. Suppose we get a paper cut in the office. In that case, we find a Band-Aid, slap it over the paper cut, and carry on while avoiding hand sanitizer like the plague.

Complaining doesn't fix anyone's problems. It certainly vocalizes them, but it also rewires your brain for negativity. Most people like to have friends who are optimistic and uplifting. Complaining creates an air of negativity, doesn't help a situation, and can turn people off.

At work, you'll notice the usual water cooler gang and their "Slackers, assemble!" daily ritual to complain about how tired they are and continually circle the proverbial drain. Please don't become one of them. If you are, seek to improve and change. Set a good example for others and stay positive.

Good leaders carry on and don't complain. They seek to fix problems and motivate others. If something's not going right in your life or you're having a bad day, try joking about it and look at the glass as half full rather than half empty. Focus on the positive aspects. Everything will turn out alright in the end.

Turning Things Around

If you're having a bad day and things spiral downward, grab a piece of paper or make a note on your phone and write a list of at least ten things that make you genuinely grateful. Gratitude can redefine a whole structure of thought, and whatever feelings you're having right now can attract the same feelings for the rest of the day.

By focusing on what you're grateful for, the hardship will wash away and you'll be more centered. When you control how you feel and stay thankful no matter what's happening, your problems won't seem so bad, and everything will start to change. Appreciate even the most minor experiences in your day today. Look for the good, and your mood will vastly improve.

You Get What You Get, and You Don't Throw a Fit

You'll often hear parents saying this to young children at the supermarket in some form or another. The same is true of adulthood. Be satisfied with what you have and remain grateful. Don't let petty jealousies or the misconception of unfairness stop you from living a happy, fulfilled life.

Go to the Library!

The library offers a vast palace of information for *free*. Are you an actor or an aspiring playwright? Check out screenplays, stage scripts, and books on writing. Are you interested in engineering, design, computer games, or architecture? Read up on all you need to know to help you along. You can also rent audiobooks, e-books, and DVDs for free. Take advantage of it.

Apartment Hunting

Getting into an apartment these days is more complicated than ever before. Prices have skyrocketed, availability is lower, and living costs have risen exponentially in the last decade alone. Unless you live in New York or an urban area where it's hard to get an apartment, steer clear of personal ads or roommate-wanted ads. Sublet rooms do not have the same assurance, safety, and free maintenance as commercial property rentals. You never know who you're getting as a roommate. The exception is if you already know the person and feel confident in your decision.

Scour the Apartment Guide website (www.apartmentguide.com) and similar sites to find an apartment that best suits your needs. Here are important questions to ask yourself:

1. How many bedrooms do I really need?
2. Does the kitchen come equipped with a dishwasher and microwave?
3. Is it affordable and in my price range?
4. Is it in a friendly, safe area?
5. Is there a nearby bus or train line? Or is it close to where I work or go to school?
6. Do they allow pets?
7. Is there a gym, laundry room, or pool? (These can cut your other membership costs.)

You can find an apartment well suited for you and your budget by tailoring your search to your specifications. The Apartment Guide website breaks down all needs and amenities. It allows you to compare other apartments you may be hunting. The more amenities an apartment complex offers, the better—it means you'll save money and that your daily life will be more convenient.

Some things to consider:

Chapter 9: Life Advice

- Do you know someone who would make a good roommate, like a close relative or friend? Having a roommate will help enormously, especially in today's economy. Having a trustworthy, dependable roommate will help cut costs in half so you don't have to struggle.
- How much is the rent deposit? Do they have a pet deposit? Make sure you have enough saved to cover moving costs, deposits, and the first month's rent.
- How will you move? Do you have friends or family who can help, or do you need to save money for a moving company?
- Do they offer student or military discounts? Usually such places will also have like-minded people your age, and it's a great way to make new friends.
- Is there covered parking? Some places charge for covered parking in the rent.
- What is the crime rate like in that area? Is it a safe place to live? Put yourself in a nice, clean area you can safely live in for at least a few years.
- Does the apartment offer different wall paint plans? Some will let you select the color of the walls at an added price.
- Steer clear of any apartment complex that looks shabby or unkempt. Are the grounds kept up regularly, and are the buildings in good repair? A decent apartment complex will always have a good repairman and custodian on site and will look clean.
- Is there shopping within walking distance?

Helpful Hint: Keep your apartment clean and in good condition. You could be charged fees for damages or uncleanliness when you move out.

Renter's Insurance

Renter's insurance protects personal possessions from events beyond your control, such as fire, theft, or natural disasters. If the worst were to happen, you would want your property insured. Renter's insurance protects against liability if anyone sustains an injury at your rental home. Check with an apartment manager or landlord to see if their insurance covers possessions, and if necessary, obtain affordable renter's insurance through a reputable insurance agency to safeguard personal belongings.

Be a Courteous Neighbor

Don't blast your music or movies at a loud volume at 10:30 at night or later. Instead, if you need to jam out, put in your earbuds or headphones and dance your head off. Just be aware that other people in the same building need their peace and sleep. Some families have babies and children, and loud music can scare them.

Fire Prevention

Half of all house fires start in the kitchen. After cooking, make sure you turn the oven or stove off. Never use the range to warm up your house or apartment. Check that you've turned off all appliances and burners before leaving home. Never leave a pot of boiling water or sizzling meat unattended, especially if a baby, child, or pet lives in your home.

Keep a small fire extinguisher handy, either bolted to a corner wall or beneath the kitchen sink. These are affordable, and you can purchase one at Walmart or Target. Never place anything flammable near the stove or microwave. It's up to you to exercise caution in the kitchen. If leaving a Crock-Pot dish to cook all day while you work, be sure it's secure on the counter and out of the way of any other electronics and flammable liquids. Stay careful and conscious of everyone's safety.

Beware of Phone and Internet Scams

There are many scams and targeted fraud these days aimed at identity theft. Do *not* engage with anyone via phone or email claiming to be from the FBI or IRS. Delete all spam emails and be wary of any aggressive callers.

The IRS and FBI are federal government agencies that would never call you asking for your personal information. You should never send money or information to someone claiming to be from a third-world country. Donate to professional organizations such as the Red Cross and the Jane Goodall Institute if you want to give charitably. The consumer protection department of the Federal Trade Commission (FTC) keeps a confidential database of all reported scams on this website: https://reportfraud.ftc.gov/. If you suspect someone is trying to target you, report it to the FTC. Protect your data online.

On Marriage

Before you decide to get married, be sure you and your spouse-to-be have a strong sense of self. People change as they get older, and it's essential to have a moral compass and grounded personality before you commit to spending the rest of your life with someone.

Age, experience, and education change people. Both you and your future spouse should have lived enough of a life that you both have a firm grasp on what the future looks like or what shape you'd like it to take together. Get an education, go on adventures together, and travel before you decide to settle down.

Other Life Advice

In life, it's important to be honest and follow through on your commitments. Trust your gut feelings and be open when you talk to others. Be friendly, but don't force it—let it happen naturally. Embrace the power to confidently and appropriately respond when the situation calls for it. Cultivate a positive mindset toward yourself, steering clear of self-criticism and negative thoughts. Chase your dreams and keep dreaming, even if you succeed. Learn to let go of things beyond your control.[20] Stay away from drama, gossip, and negativity. Choose to be kind when you talk to others.

Understand the difference between professional advice and personal opinions. Acknowledge your own worth with compassion, and aim high in your expectations. Have a backup plan ready for times when things don't go as you thought they would (i.e., "If plan A doesn't work out, I always have Plan B"). Carve out moments to take care of yourself, placing self-care at the forefront. Foster an overall sense of love, both for others and yourself.

Literary Inspiration

"If you want your children to be intelligent, read them fairy tales. If you want them to be more intelligent, read them more fairy tales."

—ALBERT EINSTEIN [20]

"Today you are You, that is truer than true. There is no one alive who is Youer than You."

—DR. SEUSS [21]

"Promise me you'll always remember: You're braver than you believe, and stronger than you seem, and smarter than you think."

—CARTER CROCKER [22]

CHAPTER 9: LIFE ADVICE

Don't Quit—A Famous Anonymous Poem

When things go wrong, as they sometimes will,
When the road you're trudging seems all uphill,
When the funds are low, and the debts are high,
   And you want to smile, but you have to sigh,
     When care is pressing you down a bit—
     Rest if you must, but don't you quit.

   Life is queer with its twists and turns,
   As every one of us sometimes learns,
     And many a fellow turns about
When he might have won had he stuck it out.
Don't give up though the pace seems slow—
   You may succeed with another blow.

     Often the goal is nearer than
   It seems to a faint and faltering man;
     Often the struggler has given up
When he might have captured the victor's cup;
And he learned too late when the night came down,
   How close he was to the golden crown.

   Success is failure turned inside out—
   The silver tint in the clouds of doubt,
   And you never can tell how close you are,
     It might be near when it seems afar;
So stick to the fight when you're hardest hit—
It's when things seem worst that you must not quit.

     —ANONYMOUS [23]

FIRST APARTMENT CHECKLIST

Living room
- [ ] candles/plants
- [ ] center table
- [ ] lampshades
- [ ] rug
- [ ] side table
- [ ] sofa
- [ ] television
- [ ] wall shelves

Bathroom
- [ ] bath towels
- [ ] cleaning supplies
- [ ] hand towels
- [ ] laundry basket
- [ ] shower curtain
- [ ] soap dish
- [ ] toilet brush
- [ ] trash can/bags

Bedroom
- [ ] bed pillows
- [ ] bedframe
- [ ] bedsheets
- [ ] blanket
- [ ] closet
- [ ] comforter
- [ ] curtains
- [ ] dresser
- [ ] mattress
- [ ] rugs

Others
- [ ] extension cords
- [ ] first aid kit
- [ ] flashlight
- [ ] scissors
- [ ] toolbox
- [ ] vacuum

Kitchen
- [ ] blender
- [ ] broom/dustpan
- [ ] dish soap
- [ ] dish towels
- [ ] kettle
- [ ] knives
- [ ] large fry pan
- [ ] large saucepan
- [ ] microwave
- [ ] mop
- [ ] mugs
- [ ] plates
- [ ] silverware
- [ ] slow cooker
- [ ] small fry pan
- [ ] spatulas
- [ ] spoon/fork
- [ ] tables/chairs
- [ ] tongs
- [ ] trash can/bags
- [ ] wooden spoons

10

"Everyone should have kids. They are the greatest joy in the world. But they are also terrorists. You'll realize this as soon as they're born and they start using sleep deprivation to break you."

—Ray Romano [24]

ALL THE SELF-HELP BOOKS IN THE WORLD CAN'T TRULY PREPARE YOU FOR being a parent. It's something you have to experience firsthand. And there's no such thing as a perfect parent or—more to the point—an ideal child. We have poop catastrophes with the babies, the babies can't figure out why we don't understand their cries, and we learn as we go along.

Despite all the craziness, children fill our lives with light and laughter. Through their sweet and innocent natures, they cement the love in our hearts when we pass on what we know to them. While every child is different, there are a few helpful things you can do to make life a little easier on the roller-coaster ride of parenthood.

Be Patient

Don't get worked up about the small stuff. Beneath the joy and unique experiences you'll encounter with your child, parenthood is the ultimate test of agility and long-suffering. Seek to be understanding and patient as you raise your child. Remember, they are innocent and on another level. They don't have the maturity of an adult or the wisdom that comes with experience. There will be mishaps and moments when it seems like your last nerve is hanging by a fragile thread. They're watching how you react to everything and absorbing it like a sponge. Be patient, laugh, and be kind.

Teach Them to Love You, Not Fear You

A home is, firstly, a place where children should be able to live in a safe, secure, and loving environment. Engender trust, respect, and gratitude through your relationship with your child. Be firm, consistent, and loving in your approach. Build happy, beautiful memories together and enjoy your time with them at all stages of their life journey.

Let Them Make Mistakes

We learn to get back up by falling. If babies are saved and picked up every time they attempt to stand up from a crawl, they will never learn to stand or walk. Likewise, a child or teenager cannot truly learn unless they're allowed to make their own choices and mistakes. Calibrate what you feel is correct and appropriate for their age, and let them learn as they make their own choices. Encourage and guide them along the way.

Embrace Your Sense of Humor

Think about the funny moments in your childhood when a parent or teacher made you laugh—how easy it was to recall that memory and that specific moment. Just like you can call it to mind, your child will remember funny things you say and do. Keep things light. Laugh a lot and create a fun nickname for your child. Childhood is fleeting and goes by very fast, so enjoy every second and make the most of it.

Share Your Talents, Skills, and Beliefs with Them

Do you play the piano, sing, or paint? Are you a skilled artisan or engineer? Do you teach Sunday School at church? Teach them what you know, and show them your hobbies, beliefs, and extracurricular passions. We pass our traits down to our kids, and it's amazing what they pick up and evolve into when their parents invest in their talents. Share what makes you happy with your children; it will bring you closer while giving them a healthy outlet.

Help! I've Been Taken Over by a Tiny Human

Parents often say that having an infant in the home is like Christmas. And it is! Babies are perfect—you wish you could bottle their fresh newborn smell. But parenthood can also overwhelm first-time parents. You must learn how to take care of them and worry about their health, and between sleep deprivation, diaper changes, and bottle runs, it's hard to know which way is up and which is down.

Here are some things to consider that can make your transition into parenthood easier:

- **Sleep deprivation—a rite of passage.** Compromise is the name of the game here. You and your partner will both feel exhausted. Remember to love each other and practice patience as you tag team through the first few months. Sleep when the baby does and enlist family and friends for advice and support. Create a bedtime routine for the baby and praise your partner for their efforts.
- **Relationship changes.** A baby cements a relationship in marvelous ways and evolves you from couple to family status. You will have to adjust and make room for your little one in your

relationship. Be compassionate with each other and lean into the changes with a glad heart, even when you feel exhausted.

- **Postpartum depression (PPD).** PPD affects 1 in 7 women and is more common than you might think. PPD can happen to anyone, regardless of lifestyle or emotional health. If you are a woman and you feel sad, experience anxiety, or have concerns about yourself or your baby, seek immediate professional help. Reaching out will make all the difference.
- **Baby blues.** Up to 80 percent of mothers experience baby blues at one time or another. However, it usually dissipates in a few weeks after birth. Baby blues are a milder form of postpartum depression and have to do with hormonal changes, which make women feel more tired and depressed than usual. If you have baby blues that don't level out, please talk to a doctor.
- **Breastfeeding.** Powerful nutrition and bonding time are only a small portion of the excellent benefits of breastfeeding. However, a vast number of women run into issues with breastfeeding for many reasons. When you first learn to breastfeed, it is more than usual to experience frustration and hardship. Consult a lactation specialist or doctor if you want to breastfeed but experience difficulties.
- **Formula feeding.** If you're not able to breastfeed, formula is a healthy way to feed your baby. There are many formulas available to tailor to the baby's needs.
- **Diapers.** You can choose from different types of diapers. Some people prefer cloth, others prefer disposable ones, and the rest go with a mix of both. Experiment with what works best for your baby, and you'll find a comfortable, easy-to-use diaper style. Babies outgrow diapers fast, so think ahead when you stock up, and get a few packs in bigger sizes when you buy newborn diapers.
- **Clothing.** Babies grow like radishes, so watch how much you spend on clothing. You can find affordable and stylish clothes at different stores. Resale stores are an easy way to upcycle a baby's wardrobe and are worth investigating. They allow you to sell gently used clothes that your baby has outgrown, then you can use in-store credit to buy newer clothes and keep cycling out. Also, never underestimate the power of hand-me-downs.

CHAPTER 10: PARENTING

- **Car seats.** Car seats are a legal requirement, and they keep babies safe. Choose an appropriate car seat for your baby's age and weight and install it correctly.
- **Strollers.** Strollers are a great way to get the baby out and about, and various strollers are available to fit your lifestyle.
- **Baby gear.** Many types of baby gear are available, from swings to bouncers to playpens. Don't buy all the equipment in one go unless you have a nest egg. A few items here and there will do the trick.
- **Social support.** If you struggle as a new parent and need assistance, reach out to family, friends, and doctors. Parenthood is a huge transition, so don't be ashamed to ask for help. There are lots of people who can help you.

Parenthood is a once-in-a-lifetime milestone. Nothing equals looking into your child's eyes for the first time or the ultimate joy and magic of having a baby. You will face challenges like every parent, but if you stay aware of available resources and prepare for what lies ahead, the transition to parenthood will feel more manageable.

Schools

Schooling for children today is quite different than it was for previous generations. There are several choices—charter schools, homeschooling, online classes, and public schools. Whatever avenue you choose, take the time to research and choose whichever seems best for you and your child. Charter schools offer tours of their schools at designated times. Information is abundant online for those interested in homeschooling. Explore all your options and make the best decision for your family's needs.

Family Memberships

If you live in or near a city, chances are they have a planetarium, zoo, aquarium, botanical garden, recreational center, or children's museum. Invest in an annual family pass if you and your family enjoy any of these activities. Yearly memberships generally cost around \$100–\$200 per family. You could go wherever you desire once a month without paying a penny after purchasing the annual pass. After the second visit, the membership would pay for itself.

Family memberships have many advantages. You can go as often as you'd like for free (even if your funds are low). You can get a significant percentage taken off purchases at gift shops. And you'll always have something to do on a rainy day or in times of financial hardship. A good part of the year to invest in annual family memberships is when you get your taxes back. Membership fees of \$200–\$300 go a long way and save you hundreds of dollars year-round on family activities. Yearly passes are also a wise investment for a young married couple.

Parks and Recreation Classes

Visit your local city or county's Parks and Recreation website. Sign your children up for swimming lessons, gymnastics, dance, sports, school programs, and seasonal summer camps throughout the city. See if there is a 4H, "Arts in the Park," or YMCA program in your state. Parks and Recreation, YMCA, and 4H are safe, licensed, and often more affordable than private instructors.

Let Your Kids Experiment

Freedom of expression and the ability to experiment helps children to build their natural personalities. If they want to dress up, let them dress up. If they request to wear mismatched outfits as toddlers, let them.

Saying No

It's okay to tell your kids no. You *should*. Suppose you fall into the trap of saying yes all the time because you love them so much and care only for their happiness. In that case, they won't learn to respect you or understand what it means to have control over their feelings. Children need their parents to teach them discipline and respect or they'll end up harming others and themselves. Care begins in the home. Do not let yourself feel guilty. Tell your child they can wait if you're trying to clean and make breakfast and get everything done at once and they're tugging on your shirttail.

As parents, we *must* have some backbone. Saying no is our leverage and gets us through day-to-day stress as a parent, but being grounded will help you maintain that calm and controlled balance. It will also help your child to learn to respect you.

Introduce Them to the Arts

Introduce music, theater, dance, and art to your child. Let them discover what they enjoy and encourage them to pursue it. Save up and go to the ballet and Disney On Ice.

Child Care Co-ops

Take advantage of co-op opportunities. Co-ops can cut childcare costs significantly while offering you an opportunity to care for yourself. Many gyms offer a crèche or co-op day care room where parents can volunteer to help for an hour in exchange for free babysitting while they work out.

Co-op Date Nights

Do you have a small group of friends you trust who also have young children? Get your friends together and talk about doing a co-op date night. The system works better with three to four families who get along and enjoy each other's company. One couple babysits all the families' kids, entertaining them while the other couples go out, and then they make the most of two date nights when the other couples take turns babysitting. Co-ops save everyone money on babysitting, and the children can socialize with other kids and have fun.

TV and Cell Phone Usage

Toddlers shouldn't be placed in front of televisions until they are at least two years old. Their overall electronics exposure shouldn't exceed more than two hours a day. Babies and toddlers need one-on-one time with their caregivers, lots of love, and external stimuli. There are many computer games for babies and productive speech therapy apps, but keep screen time to a minimum. Babies spend their first years mimicking and essentially mirroring adults.

Cultivate relationships with your baby and toddler by doing baby gym classes or spending time at the park. Tween years are a critical time for children's egos to develop. They need time to develop their personalities and character before the door opens to social media, which often tells us who we should be.

PARENT CHECKLIST
for first-time parents

EQUIPMENT

- [ ] Car Seat and Stroller
- [ ] Crib/Bassinet
- [ ] High Chair
- [ ] Thermometer

CLOTHING

- [ ] Baby Bath, shampoo, and towels
- [ ] Baby Blankets and swaddling accessories
- [ ] Baby Clothes: onesies, socks, outfits and shoes
- [ ] Pacifier

FEEDING

- [ ] Baby Formula/Breast Pump
- [ ] Bottles and bottle warmer
- [ ] Burping cloths
- [ ] Teething ring and baby-friendly toys

DIAPER DUTY

- [ ] Cream/Ointment
- [ ] Diapers (plan ahead)
- [ ] Diaper Bag
- [ ] Wet Wipes

11

Survival

"Before anything else, preparation is the key to success."

—Alexander Graham Bell [25]

Life is full of surprises. No matter how squared away you might feel, emergencies are a stark reality throughout one's lifetime. Disasters can include earthquakes, tornadoes, food shortages, pandemics, and the threat of nuclear war. Whether you're facing a natural disaster or a zombie apocalypse, nothing hits harder than being helpless.

American psychologist Abraham Maslow famously stated that our actions are motivated by specific physiological needs—food, safety, love, and self-esteem.[26] The basic requirements for our survival include food, water, breathing, shelter, and clothing. Given these fundamentals, it only makes sense to be prepared.

On Preparedness

Preparing your basic emergency needs of food, water, and essentials frees your mind to tackle the situation and stave off anxiety by already having what you need.

The Federal Emergency Management Agency (FEMA) recommends storing a minimum of 72 hours' worth of food, water, cash, emergency essentials, and medicine.[27] Here are some tips to help you prepare in an emergency.

Food

When stocking up food supplies for anything from a power outage to a pandemic, the first thing that comes to most people's minds is doomsday preppers' wall-to-wall cache. The mental cliché is overkill, but you can start food storage with healthy, cost-effective items without breaking the bank. If you think practically about food, many long-term food staples are usually quite reasonably priced.

The following items have a shelf life of two years to indefinite and are available at low prices:

- Wheat
- Rice
- Flour
- Pasta
- Beans
- Lentils
- Honey
- Olive or vegetable oil
- Soy sauce
- Canned vegetables and soups
- Canned meat (tuna, chicken, etc.)
- Peanut butter and jam/jelly
- Powdered milk
- Pasta sauce
- Dried fruit

Water

You should have at least three gallons of water at home in your storage. The rule of thumb is one gallon per person daily, so if you have roommates or children, multiply that.

Bottled water is easy to purchase at the store. Still, there are great, affordable methods of preserving water that will maintain your water supply for up to five years with the proper treatment. These are reasonably priced online and come in handy, especially for apartment dwellers. Water preservation methods include water bricks, stackable units, or fifty-five-gallon barrels you can order online. Invest in a WaterBOB or bathtub emergency water container—a fillable liner that allows you to collect water in your bathtub, giving you forty to a hundred gallons of potable freshwater in less than five minutes.

Have some way to purify water, whether it's a LifeStraw, a Britta filtering pitcher, or a gravity system water filtration you might use while camping. If you must shelter in place in a hurricane or lockdown, you will want to make sure the water you drink is clean.

Pets

Be sure you have at least three days' worth of food, water, pet supplies, medicines, and your pets' health records. Your emergency preps should include your fur babies too! Often in the fog of emergencies, pets can unfortunately be left behind.

Gas

Always keep your gas tank at least half full. If the gas stations weren't available in an emergency and you had to get somewhere fast, half a tank would only get you so far.

Emergency Cash

You should try to have at least $1,000 in emergency cash. Imagine if the power went out for an extended amount of time. You could only pay cash for gas, hotels, transportation, or groceries. You want to cohesively get these things with little to no stress, leaving you free and focused on other essential items. One way to save $1,000 over a year is to save $40 from each biweekly paycheck, or $80 a month. You will have $1,000 within a year!

Bug-Out Bag

The safest place during an emergency will most likely be your home. But in the unlikely event of a wildfire or earthquake, or should disaster strike and you need to evacuate, you will want to have a fully packed grab-and-go "bug-out" bag. A bug-out bag is a 72-hour kit filled with three days' worth of food and supplies to sustain and help you survive the disaster.

A bug-out bag is essential to help get you through the enormous stress a disaster can bring while keeping you and your loved ones alive, fed, and warm. You can find most of these supplies at the dollar store or reasonably cheap on Amazon or your local army surplus store. Here is an itemized list of what you should have in your bag:

Items for a 72-Hour Kit

- 1 gallon of water per person per day
- LifeStraw or other method to filter water
- 3-day supply of food (freeze-dried, MREs, canned foods, etc.)
- Can opener
- Cooking technology or heater
- Extra clothing and blankets
- Prescription and non-prescription medicine
- First aid kit and face masks
- Battery- or crank-powered radio
- Plastic sheet and duct tape (for shelter) or a tarp/emergency tent
- Pen and paper
- Flashlight and batteries
- Long-burning emergency candle
- Water-proof matches
- Hygiene supplies
- Pocket knife or multi-tool
- Cord or rope
- Money

CHAPTER 11: SURVIVAL

- Copies of personal documents and important information
- Games and other entertainment
- Hand and body warmers
- 3 trash bags for sanitation
- Solar-powered charger
- Toilet roll (remove paper insert)
- Baby wipes
- A laminated map of the area
- A glow-in-the-dark compass

September is national preparedness month and is an excellent time to revamp emergency supplies. Keep your 72-hour kit in an easily accessible bag and keep it updated. Make a habit of marking your calendar to update your bug-out bag and emergency supplies each September.

Longer-Term Food Storage

Ideally, it would be best if you worked up to having a three-month supply of food and financial reserve that you can live on to stay alive. Could you pay one to three months' rent or mortgage out of pocket if an EMP or solar flare took out the power? What if you lost your job? How would you and your loved ones survive? There are foods we have today that our ancestors didn't, which can last up to thirty years. These include wheat, rice, pasta, oats, beans, potatoes, and freeze-dried foods.

There is an excellent, diverse selection of dehydrated and freeze-dried foods today. While a bit higher in price, freeze-dried foods are filling, nutritious, and last up to three decades in proper storage.

First Aid Training

You can have all your preps in place and feel squared away, but supplies will do you no good without a basic knowledge of rendering first aid. If you aren't familiar with first aid, take a first aid course at your local hospital or enroll in CPR training. Knowing how to treat a light burn victim or being able to take care of someone's wound if the hospitals are full will

151

help save lives. Watch instructional videos, participate in first aid classes, and become proficient in your ability to help.

Self-Defense

Self-defense isn't just a way to know how to protect yourself and others. It's a powerful way to improve your balance and work on self-confidence, which helps you hone your internal locus of control discussed earlier in the book. Self-defense teaches you self-respect, helps you set goals, and positively influences your life as you discover a new, more assertive you. If someone attacks you, you stand a better chance of staying safe and keeping others safe by taking a self-defense class ahead of time.

Apartment Survival

An emergency preparedness room and an expensive underground bunker are all well and good for rich folks in large homes, but what about those of us who live in apartments? Apartment dwellers may have limited storage space, but never fear—this is when creativity goes to work for you.

Here are ways to keep food storage with limited space:

- Store bulky items like water bricks, canned food, and first aid kits beneath the bed.
- Store extra emergency gear in closets, and use shelves for flashlights, batteries, and tools.
- Use kitchen cabinets to store food, water, matches, and candles and possibly a portable stove.
- Capitalize on extra bathroom cupboard space to store water and foldable bathtub storage bladders, which allow you to fill up over eighty gallons of water in an emergency in less than five minutes.
- If you have a balcony storage closet or a garage, use the space to store oversized items such as camp gear, generators, and tools. Storage areas are an excellent place to keep a bug-out bag on an easy-to-grab hook. Keep emergency preparedness gear in a dry, cool place.

Make use of vertical space. Use tall, thin corner bookshelves to expand floor space and store extra food storage.

Get creative. Use baskets, bins, and old suitcases at the top of a closet to store freeze-dried food, cans, and nonperishable food storage.

Label possessions to make them easier to find in a hurry.

Rotate supplies to ensure that food and water are fresh and that batteries still work.

Test gear to ensure it's in working order.

Limited apartment space doesn't mean you have to be less prepared. Have a plan for an emergency such as a fire, flood, or other natural disaster. Ensure you know where to go in the event of an evacuation and have a way to contact loved ones. Get to know your neighbors. A network of people you trust can be invaluable in an emergency.

Keep your apartment clean and organized to locate what you need in an emergency. Have a first aid kit on hand for minor injuries or illnesses. Be prepared for unexpected expenses. Emergencies like a broken appliance or a water leak can happen anytime. Make sure you have saved enough to cover these unexpected costs.

Take note of the security features around the apartment building. Locate fire alarms, security cameras, and door locks. Test your carbon monoxide and smoke detectors regularly to ensure they work. If the power or water goes out, have a plan in place for what you'll do. Keep food and water on hand and know where to go for shelter.

Surviving a Pandemic

It's all fun and games making a joke about prepping for a disaster, until that breaking news announcement sends your stomach plummeting and your mind circling into a tailspin. March 2020 sent toilet paper, food, hand sanitizer, and cleaning wipes flying off the shelves, and people were scrambling to find items they hadn't ever considered stocking before.

Here is some practical advice for preparing for a pandemic:

Be prepared. Stock up on your food storage, water, medicine, and cleaning supplies.

- Have a good supply of five-ply face masks and disposable gloves handy.
- Disinfect the toilet(s) every day. Wipe down door handles, light switches, counters, and frequently touched surfaces. Clean the bathroom once or twice a week.
- If you live in a house, get a higher-grade virus/bacteria air filter for your home furnace, and during the pandemic, switch it out once a month. Make a note of the date you changed it on your calendar.
- Make your home the comfiest and most relaxed place to be, keeping in mind that you might have to shelter in place for two weeks to a month or longer. Invest in exercise equipment, fun board games, books, video games, movies you enjoy, and table topic conversation cards.
- Commit to learning a new skill during quarantine: play a musical instrument, bake bread, paint, draw, or write a book or play. Isolation can foster creativity, and it's an ideal time for self-improvement. Nurture your creative side and take advantage of the time.
- Keep up to date on the news but do so sparingly. Once or twice a day is plenty to stay current on what's going on. Focus on a few credible sources, but limit how much time you spend getting updates. Don't let it consume your life.
- Try to get a remote, work-from-home job. If you are already situated, you will be well positioned to get through a pandemic economically.
- Get enough sleep and take vitamin C, vitamin D, and zinc daily.
- Exercise and take daily walks if possible. Do yoga.
- Where convenient, plant fruit trees and an edible vegetable garden. Plant upside-down tomato plants or raised vegetable planters if you have a balcony or patio. Gardening is still possible if you live in an apartment.
- Keep a journal or video diary to express your thoughts, worries, and experiences.
- If needed and available, speak to a counselor through telehealth.
- Get creative about socializing. Utilize virtual meeting apps that allow free face time. Have a virtual make-your-own dish session,

Chapter 11: Survival

or invite everyone to use the same recipe at a virtual dinner party with family or friends. Check in on your neighbors.

EMERGENCY CONTACTS
(OFFICIALS)

Emergency Hotline
Mobile: _____
Telephone: _____
Email: _____

Fire Department
Mobile: _____
Telephone: _____
Email: _____

Poison Control Center
Mobile: _____
Telephone: _____
Email: _____

Police Department
Mobile: _____
Telephone: _____
Email: _____

Hospital Emergency
Mobile: _____
Telephone: _____
Email: _____

Pharmacy
Mobile: _____
Telephone: _____
Email: _____

Family Doctor
Mobile: _____
Telephone: _____
Email: _____

Veterinarian
Mobile: _____
Telephone: _____
Email: _____

Animal Control
Mobile: _____
Telephone: _____
Email: _____

Insurance
Mobile: _____
Telephone: _____
Email: _____

Afterword

THE ONLY CERTAINTY WE HAVE AS WE AGE IS THAT CHANGE IS CONSTANT. It may seem cliché, but we only have one life to live. With every curveball life throws us, it's more important than ever to keep swinging and watching the ball.

Today's choices are important because you're making decisions that will impact your future relationships and career. Every bill you pay, every right choice, and every good action you execute *matters* because it will eventually compound and pave the road for who you become and where you go in this life.

I hope this book has helped and will continue to help you as you move into adulthood. People often say, "I wish I'd known this or that when I was younger." If you take every opportunity to learn what you can when you can, you will be that much better off and ahead of the game.

Thank you for coming on this journey with me. I wish you all the happiness and success as you navigate the choppy waters of young adulthood. You can achieve *anything* if you have a good attitude and are willing to work hard enough.

You've got this. Remember, you're doing better than you think you are.

—HC

NOTES

1. "A Small Leak Will Sink a Great Ship," Coign Capital, accessed July 31, 2023, https://www.coigncapital.com/insight/a-small-leak-will-sink-a-great-ship.
2. Eric Whiteside, "The 50/30/20 Budget Rule Explained With Examples," Investopedia, last modified May 29, 2023, https://www.investopedia.com/ask/answers/022916/what-502030-budget-rule.asp.
3. See Elizabeth Warren and Amelia Warren Tyagi, *All Your Worth: The Ultimate Lifetime Money Plan* (New York: Free Press, 2006).
4. Louisa May Alcott, *Little Women* (New York: Viking Penguin Inc., 1989), 111.
5. "The only time to eat diet food," AZ Quotes, accessed July 31, 2023, https://www.azquotes.com/quote/345891.
6. "Do what you can," Brainy Quote, accessed July 31, 2023, https://www.brainyquote.com/quotes/theodore_roosevelt_100965.
7. "Do the difficult things," Brainy Quote, accessed July 31, 2023, https://www.brainyquote.com/quotes/lao_tzu_398196.
8. "Nature itself is the best physician," AZ Quotes, accessed July 31, 2023, https://www.azquotes.com/quote/561762.
9. "Beauty is when you can appreciate yourself," Brainy Quote, accessed July 31, 2023, https://www.brainyquote.com/quotes/zoe_kravitz_594484.
10. "I never travel without my diary," Brainy Quote, accessed July 31, 2023, https://www.brainyquote.com/quotes/oscar_wilde_140747.
11. "No matter what people tell you," Brainy Quote, accessed July 31, 2023, https://www.brainyquote.com/quotes/robin_williams_383827.
12. Mason Currey, *Daily Rituals: How Artists Work* (New York: Knopf, 2013).
13. Héctor García and Francesc Miralles, *Ikigai: The Japanese Secret to a Long and Happy Life* (New York: Penguin Life, 2017).
14. Judy Sheindlin, *Beauty Fades, Dumb Is Forever: The Making of a Happy Woman* (New York: Harper Perennial, 2000).
15. Roald Dahl and Quentin Blake, *Twits* (New York: Penguin Books, 1980), 9.
16. Chris Williams, *Let It Go: A True Story of Tragedy and Forgiveness* (Salt Lake City: Shadow Mountain, 2007).
17. Alanis Morissette, "Hand In My Pocket," track 4 on *Jagged Little Pill*, Maverick, 1995, compact disc.

18. Wikipedia contributors, "Hippocratic Oath," *Wikipedia, The Free Encyclopedia*, accessed July 31, 2023, https://en.wikipedia.org/w/index.php?title=Hippocratic_Oath&oldid=1166995917.
19. "Most folks are as happy," Brainy Quote, accessed July 31, 2023, https://www.brainyquote.com/quotes/abraham_lincoln_100845.
20. "If you want your children to be intelligent," Goodreads, accessed July 31, 2023, https://www.goodreads.com/quotes/14912-if-you-want-your-children-to-be-intelligent-read-them.
21. "Today you are You," Goodreads, accessed July 31, 2023, https://www.goodreads.com/quotes/3160-today-you-are-you-that-is-truer-than-true-there.
22. "Promise me you'll always remember," Goodreads, accessed July 31, 2023, https://www.goodreads.com/quotes/218377-promise-me-you-ll-always-remember-you-re-braver-than-you-believe.
23. "Don't Quit," Poeticus, accessed July 31, 2023, https://www.poeticous.com/anonymous/don-t-quit-when-things-go-wrong-as-they-sometimes-will.
24. "Everyone should have kids," SComedy, accessed July 31, 2023, https://scomedy.com/quotes/9019.
25. "Before anything else, preparation is the key to success," Brainy Quote, accessed July 31, 2023, https://www.brainyquote.com/quotes/alexander_graham_bell_387728.
26. See A. H. Maslow, *Motivation and Personality* (New York: Harper, 1954).
27. See "Planning Guides," FEMA, accessed July 31, 2023, https://www.fema.gov/emergency-managers/national-preparedness/plan.

About the Author

Haley Cavanagh is a military veteran, wife, and mother. In 2020, she won the Silver Quill award from the League of Utah Writers for *Retaliation*, the second novel in her Oceanstone Initiative sci-fi series. Haley is an alumna of Columbia College and a musical theater nut, and she loves to dive into any book that crosses her path. Haley enjoys spending time with her husband and children when she's not writing. She loves to hear from her readers and encourages you to contact her via her website or social media.

Scan to visit

www.haleycavanaghbooks.com